Advance Custom Motorcycle Painting

Dave Perewitz

Published by:
Wolfgang Publications Inc.
Stillwater, MN 55082
www.wolfpub.com

1

Legals

First published in 2008 by Wolfgang Publications Inc.,
PO Box 223, Stillwater MN 55082

The information in this book is true and complete to the best of our knowledge. All recommendations are made without any guarantee on the part of the author or publisher, who also disclaim any liability incurred in connection with the use of this data or specific details.

We recognize that some words, model names and designations, for example, mentioned herein are the property of the trademark holder. We use them for identification purposes only. This is not an official publication.

ISBN number: 1-929133-53-7
ISBN-13: 978-1-929133-53-6

Printed and bound in Canada.

Advanced Custom Motorcycle Painting

Introduction

I learned to paint by hanging around the local body shop, Tarky's Auto Body, and watching my friend and his father paint cars. I used to go there after school, or after work, and just watch. Eventually I started asking questions, but still not really painting. To become a painter I painted my own bike, a 1964 Sportster. I borrowed a Binks door-jamb spray gun, which was a good sized gun for motorcycle parts. In 1970 I took the plunge and started painting bikes in my father's lawnmower shed.

That was the start and it was trial and error from there. We used acrylic lacquer back then. By 1971 and 1972 I was doing all the paint for the local guys. A tank and two fenders was thirty five to fifty dollars. A frame, molded with tank and fenders, was about one-fifty. How times have changed. It's a whole new world of paint out there. One of the things that I learned early on was not just how to lay paint down and make it look good, I learned to diagnose and fix mistakes or problems. That was very important and a key part of my learning experience. All the schooling in the world can't make up for experience like that.

There are some important steps to becoming a good painter. You have to learn patience. Don't rush the job. Even though we are always doing things last-minute, we still take as much time as the job requires. And don't compromise the quality. Quality and time tell the story.

You also need to know the products you're using inside and out. Today I'm using nothing but PPG and the new products are second to none. What's available today, in terms of the various paints, flakes and pearls, is incredible. I'm always amazed at the range of products. The PPG Vibrance paint line has brought a whole new dimension to what you can do with color.

From 1980 to 2003 we used the same old equipment and worked out of my home made, cross-draft spray booth. We heated with heat lamps and had to be careful with the exhaust fan in the winter or it would suck all the heat out of the shop. People were amazed at the work we put out. Remember, the paint is only as good as what's under it. The preparation work is the most important part of the process. Your can have the nicest artwork out there, but if the prep work isn't right, the final job just won't look right.

Don't cut corners. Take all the time you need to get the job ready in the prep stage. When you're doing the final paint, spend the extra time sanding and reclearing, it really shows in the end.

I hope this book will help painters who have had questions about custom paint get the answers they need. When I've had paint questions over the years, I would always turn to my good friends Arlen Ness or Jon Kosmoski. They were always there with the answers. More recently, Paul Stoll from PPG has stepped up with a wealth of information. He knows the PPG product like no one else and is a great guy to work with. For help and support on a more personal level, I continue to rely on the help and support of my wife Susan, my family, and my friends.

From the Publisher

The year was 1990 and I was working my way through the motel parking lots in Spearfish, South Dakota looking for this guy named Dave Perewitz. When I found Dave he was crouched down on the ground working on this very cool, flamed, Evo with twin carburetors.

The introduction must have been OK because the next morning I was taking pictures of the Evo. That first photo shoot lead to another and another until finally Dave would automatically save one or two bikes for me to shoot for *American Iron* magazine at every Sturgis and Daytona. This was back in the day when it was hard to get top-level builders to let me shoot their bikes, because everybody wanted their custom bike in a certain very dominant Biker magazine.

From shooting David's bikes for *American Iron*, I soon began shooting the signature Perewitz bikes for a calendar named Sturgis' Best Customs. My concept for the calendar was to shoot the best of David's bikes against a recognizable Sturgis/Black Hills background. For nearly ten years now we've spent Sturgis week trying to create clean and simple photos of the bikes, and just the bikes. No chicks, just flowing sheet metal and beautiful country.

I'm pleased to say that nearly twenty years since that first photo shoot I'm still working with Dave Perewitz. Only this time the photoshoots took place at David and Susan's shop in Bridgewater, Massachusetts over the course of two separate weeks. During that time David, with help from his staff of helpers and painters, and Paul Stoll from PPG, painted the bikes you see farther along in this book.

Working with David is kind of like running a marathon. The typical day starts about 9:00 AM and rolls through lunch and a late dinner. Between those meals I tried to capture every step in the process of painting a custom bike. Sometimes I was shooting pictures of Big Ron welding extended tails on a Bagger tank, and other times I showed up early in the morning to get pictures of Jay clearcoating a tank that was painted the night before. Mostly I watched and recorded Dave and Paul as they painted the tanks, fenders and bags, and then laid out various flame and graphic designs.

Next, I created a rough layout of each how-to-paint sequence and sent it back to David for captions and text. And though it's taken a long time, I think we have a book that takes the reader into the shop and allows David to share with all those readers the many things he's learned during more than thirty years as a custom bike painter.

In closing I have to thank David, Susan and all the family and staff at the Perewitz Emporium of Custom Paint for helping in every way possible to get this project finished. Thanks also to Paul Stoll for contributing most of the first five chapters. And closer to home, thanks to two local warehouses, Lowell's in Edina, Minnesota and Pro Paint in Baldwin, Wisconsin, for helping with product photos.

Timothy Remus

FAQ with Dave Perewitz

A Lifetime of Custom Painting

One of the best known names in custom bike building, Dave Perewitz, started life as a painter. In the FAQ section that follows, Dave explains just what he's learned in 30 years of painting and building some of the world's most colorful and well known custom motorcycles.

David, how did you get started customizing motorcycles?

When I was a kid I hung out at the body shop just to watch the guys paint cars. When I

Dave Perewitz and three new customs as seen just outside Sturgis in about 1991.

got my first bike I decided to paint it myself and do a custom paint job. I managed to scrounge a little spray gun from someone and the paint job turned out pretty good. The bike was a 1964 Sportster. I painted it black metallic. The paint was a special blend that the paint shop mixed up for me. Then I went to the curtain store with my mom and we bought some lace panels. I laid the lace on top of the black and sprayed silver through the lace. Then we cleared over the top of that.

Was custom painting a big part of the work you did to bikes from the very beginning?

Yes, I was a painter first and a bike builder second. That was nice later when I started to do more bike building, because I didn't need to go find a painter like most shops do.

How did you learn how to custom paint. Did someone help you, or did you go to trade school, or what?

Because I hung around the body shop I knew a couple of guys who had done some custom painting. So I got input from them and then just started practicing. My wife, Susan, bought me my first real airbrush in 1971. It was a Pasche VL which I still have to this day. That was state of the art at the time, even Keith Hanson who does a lot of our airbrush work now, used one until a few years a go.

Anyone who remembers FXRs will also remember that the early ones came with Shovelhead engines. The red paint on Dave's rubber-mount is a candy lacquer sprayed over a white-pearl base. Panels were sprayed with neon red with simple graphics and pinstripes by Roy Mason.

Another FXR from Dave Perewitz, circa 1991, with another lacquer paint job, done this time with burgundy over a dark base.

The orange-to-red Perewitz flames closely follow the shape of the gas tank, and help to make it look longer than it really is.

What were the materials you used in the beginning, was a lot of it lacquer?

It was all lacquer, and we used Metal Flake brand paint. The candies, and clear, and all the rest were from Metal Flake.

What was it like working with lacquer?

It was easy to work with lacquer. You can fix mistakes easily. Lacquer dries quickly, which means you can sand and blend fast. It's nice to work with lacquer.

How much better are the urethane paints?

With urethanes the quality is much superior, it's a better paint and once you get used to the paint it works just as well. It was a hard transition to make because no one wanted to accept the urethanes. Once you accept them though it becomes much easier. And, it continues to get easier each year because the companies make the materials easier to blend and to use.

You are known for your flame designs. Is the Perewitz trademark flame job something that evolved over time?

Well, I still have pictures in my scrap book of my first flame job. And I always liked doing flames, flames are always in style. People were always asking for flame jobs, I've done hundreds and hundreds of flame jobs. It's one of those things where you think yours are great and then you see a set that are better, so you improve. And that happens again and again, so eventually you get them to the point where flames should be.

How do you feel about pinstripes on your flame jobs?

I like pinstripes. Keith Hanson does nearly all of them now, he does such a nice job.

How do you pick the colors?

This twin carb custom, currently owned by noted tattoo artist Don Nolan, has what we've come to call "the look." The bike exhibits David's flow and sense of motion. The paint is candy cherry sprayed over a dark base.

It depends on the color combination, and on who the customer is. There are a lot of variables.

You used to do a lot of pearl jobs, is that still the case today?

Yes. Pearls are good to use in blends and in other colors. There are more good pearl pigments available now than ever before. The mistake people make is they put too much on, more is not better with pearls. When you do too much you get mottling, the effect is kind of blotchy and not smooth looking. The improvement in pearls is incredible. The paint companies like PPG, and some of the others, have so much to offer.

When you do fades, say in a set of flames, do you spray the light colors first or the dark colors first?

In blends, generally you go light to dark-though there are exceptions. With blending it's important to get a smooth transition, almost like you can't see where one starts and the other takes over. Sometimes you add a coat of pearl to the transition area. That helps to blend the two colors together-It's like the pearl melts the two colors together.

What are the mistakes that people make when they start to do custom painting?

The two biggest mistakes they make are with

Built before Baggers were cool, or fast, Tattoo Wayne's hot rod is painted with urethane candy brandywine over a pearl base, with race-inspired graphics by Keith Hanson.

This is what happens when you take a Road King and strip off all the junk. The bike becomes an oversized FXR, painted in this case with black urethane, complimented by Keith Hanson graphics.

Built for "Joe Pro," this early right side drive bike shows off some brighter and more complex flames than those seen earlier on the twin-carb bike.

Some photo shoots are more fun than than others. Photographed outside Belle Fourche, SD, the paint here is a yellow tri-coat mix of Deltron from PPG.

the clear, they either put on too much clear or not enough.

When they do artwork, they don't put on enough clear to smooth it out, and then you can feel the edges of the artwork underneath. Or else they add so much clear that it's too thick and it gets brittle. I say, only put on as much as is needed.

Another mistake people make is they try to get too creative with colors that just don't go together. They don't know how to use them and they don't blend them in the right sequence.

How did you learn to use colors that work well together?

Trial and error.

What are some of your favorite colors for custom bikes?

I love red, yellow and white in flames. I like purple, orange, and candy red for bikes. For custom bikes I lean toward the traditional bright colors.

How many paint jobs do you do in a year?

We do 40 to 50 paint jobs per year, that includes bikes that we build from scratch.

What kind of materials do you like to use?

I have a really good relationship with PPG, and one of the advantages of that relationship is that I get to try out the newest stuff. The Vibrance™ line is a good example. That's really an awesome line of paint. I also like the new crystal pearls, they are great to work with, and the new Hot Wheels colors are very vibrant, bright, candy colors.

I talked earlier about the importance of clear. PPG makes different clears and each has a different property. Some dry faster than others and some have more shine. For some, the window to buff is very short, others have a longer window. There is a clear designed for every application. The one we like is DCU2042, it has a long window to buff, it's a high-solids clear so it fills little imperfections, and it's a high gloss product.

The underlying paint is Bright and Bold from PPG, with extensive graphics by Keith Hanson.

Do you ever leave the clear just the way it dries, without buffing?

We might if we are duping a factory paint job, but we are so used to buffing that we almost always buff the clear.

One look at this and it's not hard to understand why so many people come to Dave Perewitz to have a bike built or painted. The flames in this case are toned down a bit, no yellows or purples, just a bright red sprayed over a candy red paint job.

11

Chapter One

Shop Set Up

You Need a Booth and a Plan

Whether you're painting your first motorcycle or your tenth, you need a place do the painting. An area that's relatively free of dust, where you can keep the temperature at about 70 degrees. You need enough light so you can see what you're doing, and enough air to run the spray gun, and no fans or switches that will create a spark. You also need safe storage for the paint you have on the premises, and a plan to dispose of the excess material legally.

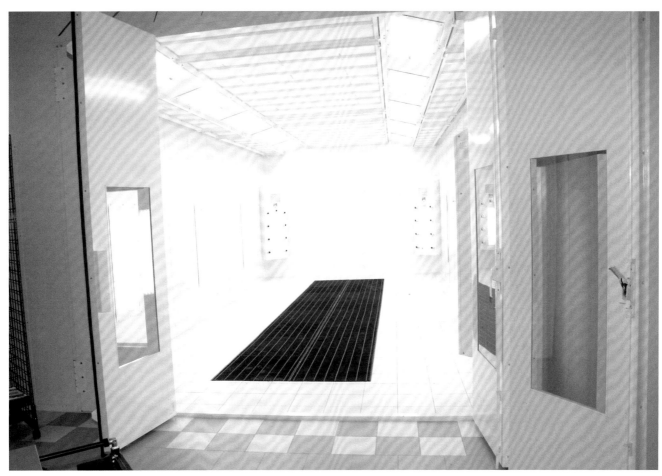

This is the Cadillac of spray booths, a new downdraft booth just installed at the Lowell's Training Center. While the individual working in a small shop is unlikely to buy something so elaborate, the things that make this a great booth apply to any booth: good air movement, good lighting, and dust and temperature control. The extra air nozzles in the corners provide additional air to help dry the new waterborne paints.

Safety and Shop Set Up

Paint overspray, paint fumes and vapors must be dealt with safely. This stuff is flammable and hazardous to use and bad for the environment. You must observe all safety rules when storing paint, mixing it, spraying it, and cleaning up your spray guns and disposing of waste.

Storage

Paint should be stored in a metal cabinet designed for flammables, with self-shutting doors. Do yourself a favor and buy fire proof cabinets to keep the paint in. Keep lids on everything, keep them tightly sealed so your product won't go bad and they won't be flammable. Drums or 5 gallon cans of thinner/solvent or paint waste should be properly grounded. Paint should be mixed and sprayed in a well-ventilated area. You should wear a paint suit to keep overspray, fumes and vapors off you and your clothes, a spray sock to protect your head and face, and a fitted respirator or fresh air system to protect your lungs. You also need non-latex, nitril gloves to protect your skin and safety glasses with side shields, or goggles, to protect your eyes.

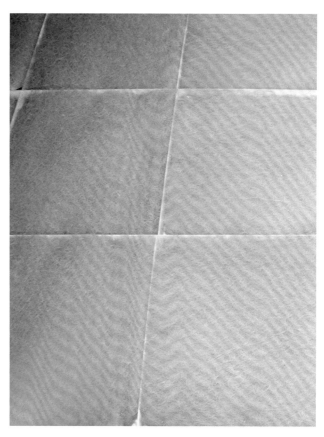

A good booth has both intake and exhaust filters. Here you see the exhaust filters on the main Perewitz booth.

The Booth

The ideal set up for Custom Painting, or any kind of kind of painting using spray equipment, is a spray booth. These can be purchased new from $8000.00 for a bare bones basic model, to $80,000.00 plus for a heated down-draft model. Often you can buy a used spray booth from a body shop, Vo Tech School, or a manufacture who is either updating to a newer model or is shutting down their painting operation. Check with your local paint stores and booth manufactures.

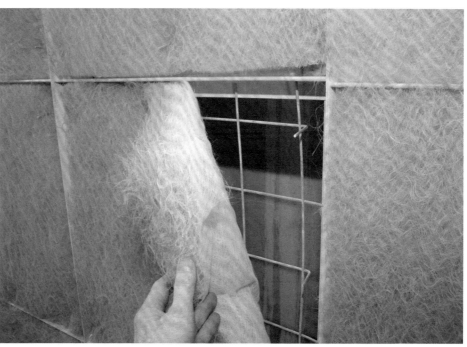

These fiberglass filters are designed to slip into the grid as shown. Note from the photo how much paint material this filter has already been captured.

The intake filters in this downdraft booth are called dispersal type, as they tend to disperse the air evenly throughout the upper air plenum so it doesn't all blow down though one small area.

Spray booths will not fit in a shop or garage with 8' ceilings, and require lots of electrical hook ups. Usually 3-phase power is required. If you don't have the space, and the price is too high, consider building a spray area. The best thing about painting motorcycles is you don't need as much space as you do for painting cars. You will need to check with your local building and fire department to see what's required.

Look at some manufactured-type spray booths to get an idea of the components and type of construction that will be required. Try to find an older cross draft type booth; you'll be overwhelmed if you look at the newer downdraft models. You don't need that type of technology anyway.

MOVE THE AIR

Your spray area needs to move air to get rid of the overspray. The air movement also helps the paint to dry through solvent evaporation. The fan you use to remove the overspray must have an explosion proof motor. It would be best to install the fan so that it pulls the overspray from the floor, this will help in cold weather to pull the warm air from the ceiling down. Remember heat rises. A box should be built around the fan to hold paint arresters/exhaust fil-

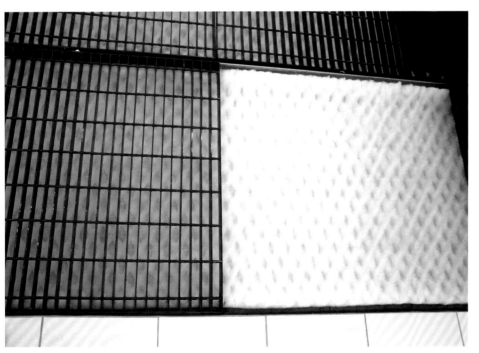

In the downdraft booth overspray exits through the series 55 filters built into the floor.

ters to trap the paint overspray so it doesn't blow out into the outside air. The air should be filtered on the way in, and the way out, of the booth. The exhaust filters are more of an open, fiberglass filter, otherwise they plug up with paint too quickly. The intake filter is typically a finer mesh, you want to filter out everything possible. Automotive paint stores are the best place to buy the filters as you will get the right quality. You will have to design the booth to fit the media or filters, some are standard rectangular sizes. If you're building a booth, look first at what is available, and in what sizes, so you can just pop those in once the booth is built. Some filters are available in rolls, so the size of the opening isn't as important. Any paint jobber should be able to help you out. They may not stock the filters but will have the resources to help you decide where to buy them (there are resources on the Sources Page as well).

A variety of intake and exhaust filters are available for your spray booth. Most come in a large roll, or pre-cut rectangular panels like those shown here, which can slip into fabricated doors or wall sections in the booth.

HEAT WITH CAUTION

You need to maintain a minimum temperature of 60 degrees in the booth, as that is the metal temperature of the parts you are painting. So if you live in a cold climate you'll need heat for your spray area. Do not put a heater of any kind in the spray area, or anywhere paint fumes,

For all sanding and grinding operations you need at least a pair of safety glasses and a dust mask.

vapors or overspray are present. Heat the air before it's drawn into the booth. If the fan draws air from an adjacent room, that's where the heater should be. Put the heater up high and draw through an intake filter to keep dirt out of your wet paint. The intake filters are also available from automotive paint stores. The last thing your paint area needs is a lot of light so you can see what you're doing. The light fixtures should be mounted so that they are sealed up in the paint area and are accessible from the other side. You can buy explosion proof lights to hang in the area, but they are not cheap. Which brings us to the danger of any electricity in the spray area. No electrical outlets, extension cords or anything that can spark should ever be present where paint fumes, or vapors are present. Go into a dark room and pull a cord out of an electrical outlet. You'll see what I mean. Take a room that's full of fumes from painting, turn on a light switch or pull apart an extension cord - and bang! You never want to convert your attached garage into a spray booth.

SAFETY GEAR

There are lots of companies that make great safety gear and can be purchased at any automotive paint store where you buy your paint.

I know, all the cool painters you've seen don't wear all that stuff, remember that doesn't make it right. Paint is very safe to use if you protect yourself properly. Safety is your responsibility.

Eyes

Wear safety glasses when handling wet paint
Wear goggles when cleaning equipment
Flush eyes with water if splashed.

2K spray mist can irritate eyes. Use a visor type mask or a full-face mask to reduce risk of irritation.

Inhalation

In areas like spray booths the correct, properly fitted, respirators are required.

Booth ventilation must be designed, maintained and operated correctly.

It is best practice to use a full-face, air-supply respirator for all spraying operations as this prevents the inhalation of any, and all, spray mist in the operating environment.

An air-fed, half-mask used in combination with safely glasses is also an acceptable form of protection. A mask must be worn when sanding.

Skin

Wear you paint overalls with hat or hood to protect yourself and your job. Use rubber gloves for protection against solvents and barrier cream before starting work. Remember, hand cleaner, not thinner, is the ticket for clean hands.

Painting with non-catalyzed paints requires a mask like that shown. Be sure the filters are designed for painting. Some of these are disposable and some use replaceable cartridges, but none of them last forever.

COMPRESSOR, SIZE AND OPERATION

You've got to have air to run the equipment. If you want to be able to run air tools and spray guns, don't go cheap on the air compressor. Don't look for horsepower, look for "Cubic Feet Per Minute" of the pump. To run spray guns you need to be above 12 CFM, and air tools need more than that. When it comes to compressors, the more the better. Too often, a guy buys a 5 hp compressor and it's 8 CFM. He can't do anything with that piece of equipment except burn it up trying to do something. If you have the money, a rotary compressor is best,

A compressor produces air and water-water you don't want. You don't want it in your air tools, and you don't want it in the air supply to the spray gun. So to properly remove the water

Some airbrush artists don't use a mask because "there's so little paint being applied." Yet the material is toxic and you need to protect your lungs.

you have choices. The most economical way is to run 25 feet of airline our of the air compressor. That airline should be not less than 1 inch ID. If you can afford bigger, go for it.

The reason you need 25 feet is that it takes that distance for the hot compressed air to cool. Moisture forms when the air cools. Now you can trap the moisture, because it's not in suspension with the air. To remove the moisture you need a moisture trap, or filter, at the end of the 25 foot run.

If you are in a garage, you can run the airline back and forth on the wall. Use copper or brass, this lets the air cool the quickest. Black pipe should be avoided. PVC doesn't cool well, and gets brittle over time and breaks. Fire departments make people get rid of the PVC.

For spraying with catalyzed paints you need a fresh air hood with it's own air supply, as shown, and a complete painter's suit.

Because the new HVLP spray guns require more air, you need air lines with a 3/8 inch inside diameter, not the old 5/16 inch lines.

This is the elaborate filter and drying rack on the outside of a new spray booth. Smaller filter/dryer set-ups are available for the home-based shop.

When you run the air-lines the airline should angle up so moisture goes back toward the compressor. The biggest mistake people make is to run the airline like a plumber does, down hill. They should "T" off the top of the line, then drop down to a fitting. And wherever there is a drop there should be a drain.

The other way to do it is to take 25 feet of 3/8-inch hose and put it in the cooler full of ice. Now put the moisture filter on the end of the hose. The hottest time of year is when you have trouble with moisture in your line. The problem using a long air hose is it doesn't cool very well without the ice. No matter how you run the airline, remember to drain the tank every night.

DISPOSAL

When you're all done you'll have paint and thinner to dispose of. This is Hazardous Waste. You'll have to check with your local landfill and see what they will let you, as a homeowner, dispose of. Body shops and business cannot use a landfill to dispose of their hazardous waste. Some shops have recyclers, and have hazardous waste picked up by licensed haulers. What you CAN NOT do is let it evaporate into the air, or pour it into the ground.

Hazardous waste must be disposed of properly, check, with your county. Be careful whom you hire to dispose of your stuff, if they are sloppy, or illegal, you could get into trouble.

No matter how carefully you plan, there are going to be leftover materials. And although it's tempting to just dump a small amount of paint out behind the garage, small amounts add up, and soon the material finds its way into the water table.

You could also ask your buddy at the body shop to let you add your wastes to his, for pickup by the licensed disposal company that picks up at any commercial operation. Considering, however, that the body shop pays by volume, and is responsible for all the wastes they generate, this might not be as easy as it sounds.

A better idea is to contact the Local Environmental Office. Usually a county function (in some cases the office is run by the city or township), nearly every community in the USA has a Local Environmental Office. Paint materials are considered HHW (Household Hazardous Wastes), and the Local Environmental Office will be able to direct you to the closest HHW collection site or provide a local information phone number. So don't let the stuff accumulate in the back corner of the garage. When the job is over, take all the leftover materials (preferably in their original containers) to the HHW collection site.

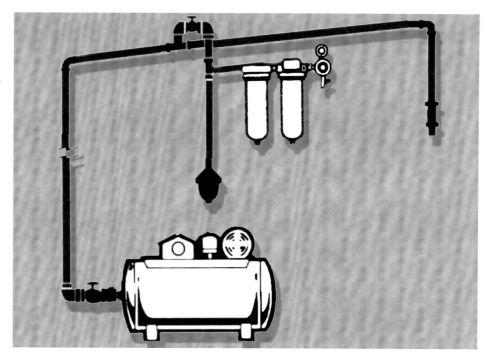

You want the air hose in the shop to be of a large enough diameter, you also need to think about the design and layout of the pipes or tubing. Each drop should turn up, and then come back down, as shown so dirt and moisture are less likely to find their way into your spray gun.

Companies like Northern Tool and Equipment sell a whole range of compressors. Don't use horsepower alone as a means of judging the capacity of a compressor. Read the tags and be sure you buy enough CFM to run your spray gun and the power tools in the shop.

Chapter Two

Modern Paint

What it is

It turns out that paint is made up of four major components: Pigments, Resin, Solvents, and Additives. Let's start by taking a look at each component (more information on these essentials can be found farther along in this chapter.

PIGMENTS

Pigments are finely ground powders: some are naturally occurring minerals, others are synthetically produced.

The pigment provides:

*Color and special effects

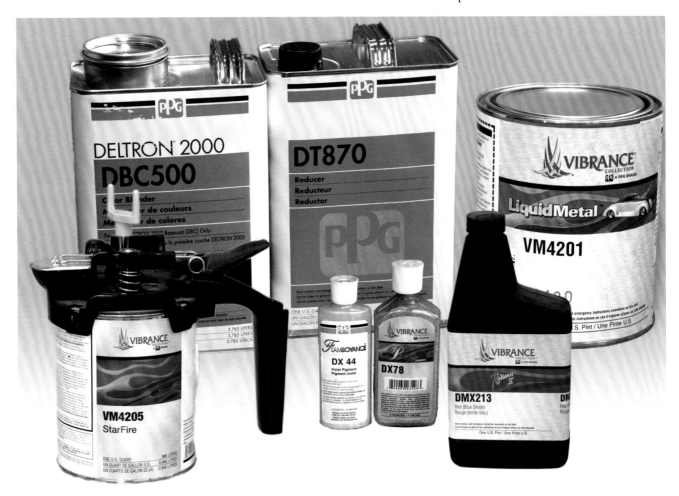

For the custom painter, there are currently more great products on the market than ever before. From intercoat clear to a huge variety of pearls, flakes and candy colors. If you don't find what you want you just aren't looking hard enough.

*Opacity (coverage/hiding power)
*Filling properties
*Sandability
*Adhesion
*Durability and corrosion resistance

RESIN

Resin is the backbone of paint, this is what gives the paint its strength.

Resin is essential for:
*Film forming
*Pigment binding
*Durability
*Gloss
*Rheology (viscosity)
*Adhesion

SOLVENTS/THINNERS

*Reduce viscosity
*Change speed of dry/flash off

Paint, whether it's old skool lacquer or new urethane, is made up of four basic components.

ADDITIVES

These are materials added to paint in small quantities to give or improve certain specific characteristics.

These characteristics include:
*UV Absorbers – Durability
*Flow additives – Leveling
*Anti-settle agents
*Driers and catalysts
*Plasticizers
*Anti-foaming agents

VOLATILE ORGANIC COMPOUNDS (VOC)

VOC is a class of materials that includes most evaporative solvents used in automotive refinish products. The largest release of VOCs at a collision center occurs when spraying automotive paint products. These compounds react with sunlight, auto exhaust, and dust to cause photochemical air pollution… better known as smog.

Where is V.O.C. Found?

V.O.C.	V.O.C.	
Resin		V.O.C.
Pigment	Resin	
Paint/ Undercoat	**Catalyst/ Hardener**	**Solvent**

Illustration shows the relative amount of VOC in the various components found in paint and paint components.

VOC is found in nearly all refinish products used in a collision center. The nearby graphic gives a basic look at each type of product in a refinish system and shows that each one contains VOCs. The graphic is not to scale but a representation of what goes into each type of product.

HOW IS REFINISH VOC MEASURED?

VOC content is measured in pounds of VOC per gallon. The most important measurement is the VOC content as applied. VOC information for PPG products can be found on the product bulletin, both for the product itself, and when it is mixed and ready to spray (RTS).

On September 11, 1998 a new national VOC regulation was put into effect that regulates the VOC level as applied for refinish paint products. Automotive refinish manufacturers can only sell undercoats, topcoats and clearcoats that meet the law. Some states and counties have enacted VOC regulations that are more strict than the national rule. Technicians must follow the regulations in their area.

THERMOPLASTIC VS. THERMOSET FILMS

The vast majority of automotive refinish paint products can be divided into 2 basic resin types, thermoplastic and thermoset. The nearby table below shows the key characteristics of each type.

Some products (a lot of aerosols and 2K etch primers) exhibit characteristics of both types listed below and can be classified as "mild thermoset" because they have thermoset characteristics but do not crosslink like urethanes.

Thermoplastic and thermoset products do not always work well together. If the chosen products

Thermoplastic	Thermoset
• Will reflow with heat or solvent.	• Will not reflow with heat or solvent.
• Cures by release of solvent, no chemical crosslink occurs. This means there will not be a "pot life."	• Cures by a chemical cross-linking between the product and a catalyst. This means there will be a "pot life."
• Generally less favored due to reduced retention of initial gloss, lowered long term durability, and increased film shrinkage during curing cycle.	• Are favored because they provide greater gloss retention, durability, and very little film shrinkage after reaching a cured state.
• Considered "1K" products.	• Considered "2K" products.

Most paint can be categorized as either thermoplastic (lacquer) or thermoset (modern urethane). The key is to know which type of paint you are dealing with before you begin to repair or repaint.

are not compatible, wrinkling or lifting can occur. Always stay within the compatible topcoat recommendations found on the product bulletins.

RESIN RULE TEST

The steps below will quickly determine if the paint film or substrates are thermoplastic or thermoset in nature.

Soak a clean cloth in a medium grade lacquer thinner. Lay the soaked cloth on the paint film/substrate for approximately 5 minutes, then rub gently. Lacquer thinner is a very strong solvent and will cause a thermoplastic to soften or dissolve. A weak or aged film/substrate may wrinkle, lift or deteriorate quickly. Check the test area for any signs of such deterioration.

If no effects are noted, the substrate could be considered sound and is most likely a thermoset film/substrate.

CONCLUSION

If the films/substrates are thermoset, the repair procedure can proceed as normal.

If a film or substrate is in any way unsound, sand it down to a sound surface, or strip it to a bare substrate before proceeding with any repairs or refinishing.

If a technician is the least bit unsure of an OEM, or refinish paint film on repair areas or replacement panels, this test should be performed.

Lacquer paints were the mainstay of custom painting for years and years. However, lacquers are currently hard to find, and illegal to use in some states. Catalyzed urethane is the new custom paint religion. These paints have color and durability that lacquer can't even touch. And they get easier to use every year.

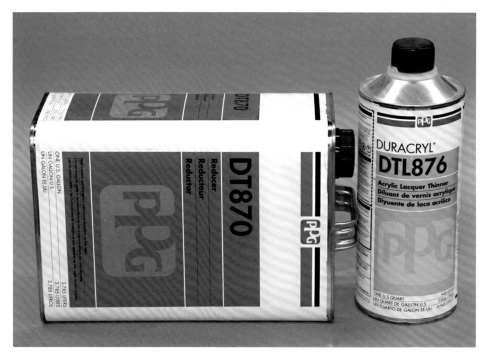

Lacquer is "thinned" to a viscosity that's easy to spray. Urethanes by contrast are reduced, with the recommended reducer chosen for the shop temperature and painting situation.

Standard Conditions:

Temperature	68-70° F / 20-22° C
Relative Humidity	50%
Air Flow	Adequate to quickly and continuously remove all overspray during application and enhance the curing process. Recommended airflow rate is between 60 and 100 FPM.

Most painters know enough to check the temperature in the booth, but it's important to know the humidity and the airflow as well.

Examples:

	60°F	Standard Conditions	85°F	100°F	115°F
Dry Time	60 min.	30 min.	15 min.	7.5 min.	3.75 min.
Pot Life	120 min.	60 min.	30 min.	15 min.	7.5 min.

Note: All product cross linking and curing in 2K products slows significantly or stops below 60°F / 16°C. Thermoset paint will not cure properly if subjected to cool temperatures during the curing stages. Such conditions can result in a finish that may eventually dry, but will exhibit reduced durability, gloss, and repairability. This loss of performance is due to the film never reaching a fully cured state.

You have to pay attention to the temperature in the booth both during and after applying a two-part paint product. Think twice before turning off the heat at night in order to save on the fuel bill.

STANDARD CONDITIONS

Standard conditions are temperature, humidity and air flow data under which an automotive paint products dry time, cure time, pot life and all general performance characteristics are determined. This information is typically found on all product sheets. The conditions used by PPG (and most refinish paint manufacturers) are as follows:

Temperature: 68-70 degrees F. Relative Humidity: 50%. Air Flow: Adequate to quickly and continuously remove all overspray during application and enhance the curing process. Recommended airflow rate is between 60 and 100 FPM (feet per minute).

THE 15-DEGREE RULE

This rule pertains to thermoset (2K) products and explains how temperature can affect a product's dry time and pot life. This rule is made up of 2 parts:

For every 15 degree increase in temperature above standard conditions, a refinish product's dry time and pot life may be reduced by 1/2. For every 15-degree decrease in temperature below standard conditions, a refinish product's dry time and pot life may be doubled.

Note, cross linking and curing in 2K products slows significantly or stops below 60 degrees F.

Thermoset paint will not cure properly if subjected to cool temperatures during the curing stages. Such conditions can result in a finish that may eventually dry, but will exhibit reduced durability, gloss and repairability. This loss of performance is due to the film never reaching a fully cured state.

WINDOW RULE

This is a simple rule, but can be dangerous if you miss the appropriate "window." This rule has three parts, and applies to thermoset (2K) coatings, and the "windows" open in the order explained.

Opportunity

Chemically soft enough to accept a subsequent coat of the same product or a compatible product. Considered to be a "wet on wet" application of the products.

Danger

Not chemically soft enough to accept and not hard enough to resist possible wrinkling that could be caused by subsequent coating.

Stability

Chemically hard enough to resist possible wrinkling that could be caused by a subsequent coating. The time necessary for each product to move from one window to the next will vary from product to product. Follow the re-coat time on all product information bulletins. Make sure to note the pot life of the product to anticipate when cross-linking will occur at your temperature. Remember the 15 degree rule applies to these times.

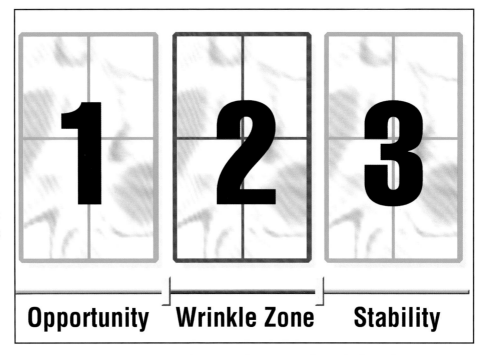

Each 2K product moves through these three stages as it cures. The trick is to understand each stage for each product you are using. These stages are not set in stone and are affected by the shop conditions, including temperature.

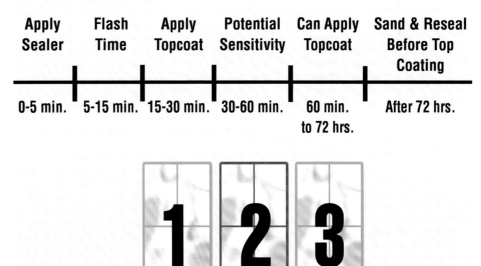

This illustration shows the two correct windows for topcoat application of a sealer product applied in a 70 degree shop. Be sure to follow the re-coat time on all product information bulletins, every product is different.

SOLVENTS/REDUCERS/THINNERS

Most automotive refinish undercoats and topcoats require the addition of a solvent. The amount and type of solvent needed can be found in the product bulletin.

A few fundamental facts need to be understood by technicians regarding solvents:

Reducers are made up of a combination, or blend, of solvents that provide different performance and application characteristics.

Reduce the viscosity of a high solids resin.

The solvents evaporate at different rates during the application process.

Alter the product's application characteristics.

Reducers are temporary tools needed during the paint application process.

The ability to correctly chose, use and understand reducers is a necessary skill for any refinish technician.

There are three primary jobs that a reducer must perform:

Make the paint thin enough to apply easily through a spray gun.

Control the flash, so all the solvents evaporate at the same time.

Allow the paint to achieve final leveling and begin the drying/curing process.

The three primary jobs listed above are performed by the three blends of solvent used to make a reducer, front-end solvents, middle solvents, and tail solvents. The nearby chart shows each of these blends and their role in the refinish process.

Type	Role
Front-end solvents	Thin the resins in the paint product to allow it to be applied with refinish spray equipment. Evaporate quickly after leaving the spray gun.
Middle solvents	Remain with atomized paint to provide initial adhesion and leveling of product once it reaches the substrate. Evaporate quickly after reaching the panel.
Tail solvents	Remain with the applied product to finish the leveling process (flow) as well as insure chemical adhesion to previous products. Evaporate last during the drying/curing process.

It's important to have a good understanding of the temperature range and evaporation rate of the solvents. This will make it easier to choose the correct reducer for a give product and set of conditions.

USE AND UNDERSTAND MODERN PAINT

MODERN PAINT

There are all types of automotive paint chemistries to choose from. Today's custom paints are urethane technologies. There are Single stage urethanes that are catalyzed with a hardener to provide fast dry, long term durability, good gloss, chemical resistance, and chip and scratch resistance. These are usually sprayed as solid colors only-black, white, red, and all the rest. Single stage urethanes are rich in resin to provide the gloss, and low in pigment, the color, so they may require more coats to get coverage.

They require overnight drying at 70-degree temp. before taping and two toning. Single stage urethanes are medium to high solids, which means the film build is pretty thick when taping, and spraying flames or graphics. This type of paint is usually reserved for painting frames or parts that may not match the custom job on the tins. This type of paint can be used as a base for your custom job. For example, you would paint all your tins with a single stage black like DCC 9300 concept black. Then, let it dry and sand with 600 – 800 grit sandpaper, lay out your flames, next spray them

Two stage urethane paint uses a basecoat and a clearcoat. The basecoat is a highly pigmented product that dries fast with a dull finish. The shine, and the protection, come from the clearcoat. Be sure to use recommended clear on the basecoat.

To shoot a single-stage urethane you need the paint, the catalyst and the reducer. By staying with the same brand all the wat through you avoid surprises and reactions between one layer or stage of the paint job, and another.

27

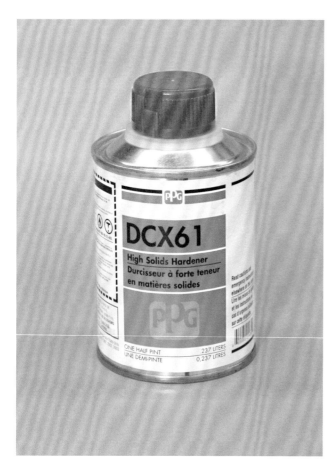

Most urethane catalysts are isocyanates, and should be handled and sprayed with care. Follow the directions and always use the correct catalyst.

bond as long as a slow enough reducer is used and a medium to wet coat is applied.

Base coats are made up of urethane resin, are pigment rich to provide faster color coverage, less resin because the gloss comes from the clear coat. Base coats are low solids so tape edges, when doing flames and graphics, are "thinner" by 1/3 than they would be if you used a single-stage urethane. This means the edges can be buried by the clear coat much faster.

A typical custom job on a tank can go from a sealer to a basecoat color, a pearl containing a mid-coat of base, a basecoat of clear to protect the midcoat from tape marks, taping graphics and applying multiple transparent candy coats of different colors, all without having to sand between colors or applying a top coat clear between colors. This could all be completed in a day depending on how involved the masking sessions are.

with base coats, then clear the entire part. Single stage urethanes are a thermoset resin that require an additive, usually a type of isocyanate hardener. This is what causes the resin to crosslink and creates the durability. Thermo set resins will not reflow with solvent once completely cured. Thermo set resins must be sanded before more paint can be applied– once cured. Thermo set resins require 16-24 hour dry times, so thermo set resins are not the fastest to work with when doing multi-color custom paint jobs.

Basecoat is the choice for custom work. Basecoats are thermo plastic resins– unless a hardener is added. A thermo plastic resin will reflow with solvent after it has dried. This means multiple colors/coats can be applied on top of each other without having to sand for adhesion. The reducer used in the base coat has the ability of softening the previous coat to give a chemical

Basecoats tend to come in solid colors, many of which can be used as the foundation for a custom paint job.

Base coat is the fastest way to apply multiple colors and effects if the proper techniques are used.

Tips for using PPG DBC/Global Base Coats
Colors – Solid vs. Pearl/Metallic and Transparent Colors

Solid colors, black, white, yellow, and the rest, are used for base coats followed by a midcoat containing special effect pigments like; pearls, Crystal Pearls, Liquid Crystal Pearls, Flamboyance, and Luminescence.

Pearl and metallic containing colors (like pearl white, silver metallic, gold metallic, blue metallic or blue pearl, red pearl) are good base coats for transparent midcoats like, Radiance II, Prizmatique, and Big Flake.

Airbrushing Base Coat

Solid colors, like white work well as highlights and are a great base for mural work. Black is great for tight detail work. Flesh tone colors and other solid colors also work well. To add depth and transparency to your work, transparent toners or Radiance II colors work the best. Be careful airbrushing Radiance II over white. Some of these colors will bleed if they are applied too soon, or too wet.

Transparent pigments (Deltron DMD1610, DMD 1675 or Global)

Raw flake is available in various colors and sizes, and is typically mixed with DBC 500 or topcoat clear. Be sure to note the application tips for flake use in this chapter.

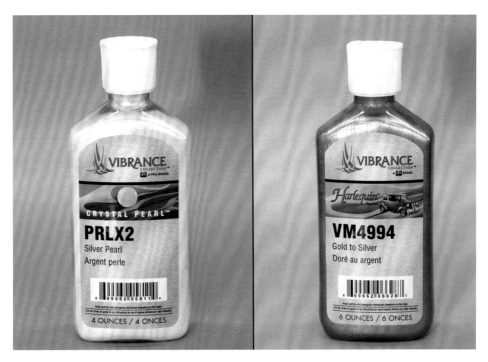

The Vibrance line includes an ever-expanding group of colored and color-shifting pearl products.

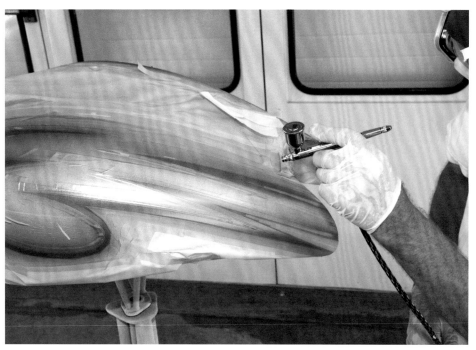

Nearly all automotive paints can be reduced to be applied with an airbrush, a very creative tool that can be used to achieve detail that will separate your graphics from all the others.

don't bleed like the dyes in Radiance II. Pearls and other special effect pigments can add nice ghost effects to your work when viewed at different angles.

CATALYZING BASE COAT

To add hardener to the base coat or not, that is the question. Before deciding, consider:

Catalyzed base coats provide a tougher film of resin. Catalyzed base coats make repairs easier. Catalyzed base coats maintain a window in which you must clear coat.

Catalyzed base coats increase tape times over non-catalyzed.

REDUCERS - SOLVENT CHOICE CAN MAKE OR BREAK YOU.

Dry time to tape is affected by your choice of a reducer.

When slower reducer is used, the job will dry-through faster. Fast reducer will skim over and appear dry on the surface, but will trap solvent underneath and still be wet. This causes tape marks and peeling. Slower reducers aid in adhesion. For airbrushing, slower reducers again will help with adhesion and prevent dried paint on the needle and cone of the airbrush.

BASE COAT TIPS FOR CUSTOM PAINTING

Spraying Technique – Light vs. Heavy Coats

Thin paint dries faster than thick paint. Avoid heavy wet coats. Heavy

Reducers come in medium (on the left) and slow part numbers, and should be chosen for the temperature and shop conditions.

coats can bleed under tape. Heavy coats can move metallics and airbrushed colors.

Heavy coats cause tape marks and longer tape times. Choose paint guns with smaller fluid tips to avoid heavy coats and improve atomization, which will improve coverage. Never spray light DRY coats, you'll get minimal adhesion. Spray medium wet coats!

INTERCOAT CLEAR – DBC 500/D895

Basecoat resin not a topcoat clear. This product makes a great "wet bed" to spray down first over a sanded finish before airbrushing, it eliminates overspray patterns and sand scratches.

Intercoat clear helps with adhesion on OEM surfaces that have been taped, then scuffed. It also protects base coat from bleeding through and prevents tape marks when applied first. Intercoat clear can also be used to protect airbrush work. Remember, you don't need to apply a heavy wet coat.

A product like DBC500 will soften a basecoat that has dried more then 24 hours and help with adhesion (when it is not catalyzed) before applying more base or clearcoat. It also helps to flow out tape marks and tape edges before applying a top coat of clear.

DBC 500 is also used as the resin to mix Vibrance Custom Colors in: Radiance II, Luminescence,

Custom paint jobs involve multiple layers, which are then buried in multiple coats of clear.

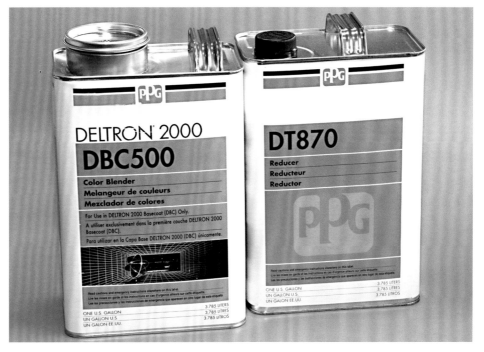

Intercoat clear and reducer, as shown, is used to protect one layer of paint or artwork from the next. Pearls and flakes can also be mixed with intercoat clear as a midcoat which is later topcoated.

31

Pearls, Crystal Pearls, Liquid Crystal Pearls, Harlequin, Flamboyance, Prizmatique and Big Flake. DBC 500 can also be mixed with DMD 1600 or Global D895 with series toners to make them more transparent for airbrushing and custom painting.

DBC 500 is mixed 1:1 with any Deltron reducers. D895 is mixed 1:1 with any D series reducer in th Global line. Spray 1-2 coats. Do not spray more than needed.

Do not use DBC 500/D895 to build and level edges when custom painting. Use a top coat clear to fill and sand edges smooth like VC5200.

BASE COAT COLORS USED FOR CUSTOM PAINTING

There are many great colors used on new cars today at the OEM level. There are a lot of pearl colors and even candy apple looking finishes. While these colors look really good by themselves, when you try to put different ones together, or add a Vibrance custom color, the OEM color tends to look a little dirty. Be careful when choosing OEM colors to be sure they will all work together.

The PPG Vibrance line has a lot of pearls that can be added to DBC 500 / D895, or mixed with a Radiance color. Pearls don't mix well with solid type colors such as white, red, and yellow. Black is the exception to this. Carbon is used as the pigment in black and it is transparent enough for the pearl-effect to show.

Pearl midcoats are sprayed over a solid color to create a pearlescent color. White is the most popular choice, however all colors will work. There are many different colors of pearls from silver/white, gold, red, violet, blue, and green. These can be mixed over different base colors for a wide range of effects.

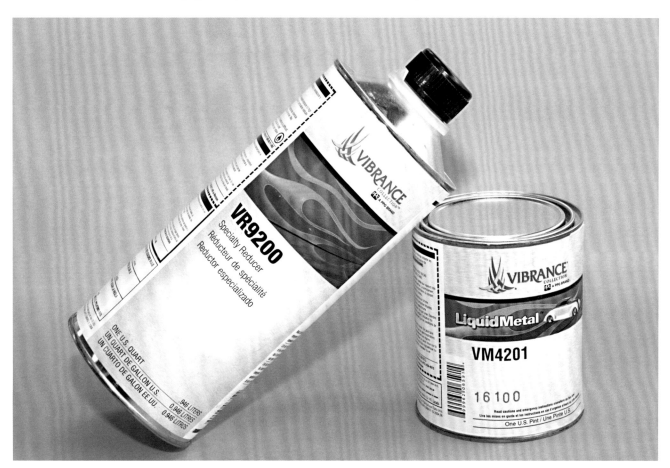

Liquid metal takes up where silver basecoat left off. This silver, made up from a very finely ground pigment, makes a great base for a candy job.

The most popular would be a silver/white pearl over white. While this looks good by itself it also makes a great base for candy colors. Black makes a great base with lots of pearl for a candy red or a black cherry. Pearls also will work over a silver metallic or any other metallic color with a more subtle effect. There are endless combinations, so have fun creating.

All the pearls in the PPG Vibrance line are packaged dry and can be mixed with any Deltron or Global basecoat color, or DBC 500/ D895 Clear. They can also be mixed together like a Crystal Pearl and Flamboyance. Just remember don't mix them with white or any other solid color.

THE PEARLS IN THE PPG VIBRANCE LINE

PRL pearls are the standard mica type pearls used in OEM colors. They have a dirty side tone

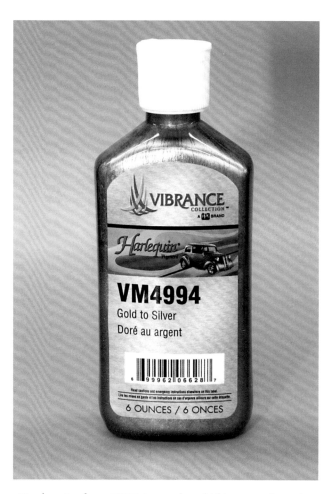

Harlequin from PPG is a color-shifting pearl product...

...that can be mixed with DBC 500 or topcoat clear, as seen in Chapter Nine.

to them, which is most noticeable when used over white.

PRLX Crystal pearls are Aluminum Oxide type pearls also used in OEM colors. They are much cleaner than the mica pearls and sparkle more in the sun. They are used in many Vibrance custom color Formulas.

Flamboyance pearls are much larger and sparkle more than Crystal pearls. These are great mixed in black or sprayed over black. These are used in the Vibrance Flamboyance Custom formulas.

Liquid Crystal pearls are color shifting and come in 4 colors. Emerald - gold to green, Emberglow – yellow to red, Caspian – green to blue, and Glacier – blue to violet. These all have a green flop to them. These are used in Vibrance colors such as "is it green", "key lime," "o- so-orange" and many other's. They have a fair amount of sparkle in the sun.

Luminescence pearls are also color-shifting pearls that come in four colors. They are much finer and have less sparkle than the Liquid Crystal pearls.

Harlequin is a special pigment that shifts through the color spectrum. Harlequin comes packaged in resin and can be sprayed as-is with hiding in 3 coats, or added to DBC 500D895 and sprayed as a mid coat over black or other dark colors. Transparent tints, or Radiance II dyes, can be added to create new colors that do not shift through the color spectrum as much.

Ditzler Big Flake is offered in various versions in the PPG Vibrance line. All these are offered dry and can be mixed with different PPG paints. The biggest flakes are found in silver and gold. Since it is very hard to get complete coverage from big size metal flake, silver should be sprayed over a silver metallic and gold over a gold metallic basecoat. The Big Flake is mixed in DBC 500/D895, or in a top coat clear. It take 4 to 6 coats to get a covered look and the flake should be sprayed wet so it will lay down, a top coat clear works best for this. Metal flake has a very rough finish and requires clear coating before taping for graphics or flames. Three to four coats of top coat clear are then sprayed over the flake and left to dry before sanding flat with 500 - 600 grit sandpaper. The metal flake is now ready for more painting or the final clear.

Prizmatique is a smaller flake that is much easier to apply. It has a rainbow look. This is used in Vibrance Prizmatique custom colors.

There are four color changing metal flakes that are sprayed over black. They spray easily and are smaller then they appear.

Radiance II is PPG's candy apple finish in the Vibrance Line. These are transparent basecoats mixed with DMX Dyes and DBC 500 / D895 basecoat clear. Candy apple colors are sprayed over a metallic or pearl containing basecoat.

Light travels through the candy coat and reflects off the pearl, metallic or flake to give a deep rich color. Adding a pearl or flake into the candy coat kills the effect, as does spraying a pearl over a candy paint job. Candy colors blend well into each other for perfect fades. Candy colors are the most chromatic over a white/pearl base. Silver and gold metallics are pretty much stan-

Meant to be mixed with clear or transparent colors, the Liquid Crystal pearls come in four color shifting "colors," gold to green, yellow to orange, blue to green, and blue to violet.

34

dard, along with the silver and gold flake, as a good base for candies. The color changing pearls, flakes, and Harlequin make good bases, but be warned as the light rays are filtered as they travel through the candy topcoat which diminishes the color shift. Luminescence colors and similar colored metallic make for a nice candy job that is much easier to spray. Candy apple paint is not the easiest to spray. Motorcycles are much easier to paint than the side of a car and those big long, flat hoods. Streaking, uneven color, mismatched parts and dirt specs that seem to get bigger as you paint are common problems with this type of finish. When done correctly nothing beats the vibrant deep look of a candy apple finish. When starting out, a similar colored base is much easier to spray. For example, pick a blue pearl or a blue metallic color for a candy blue paint job. Less coats of the candy blue will be required to achieve the color. A black base with pearl is also forgiving. Pearl white is the most difficult. Take your time when spraying a candy job.

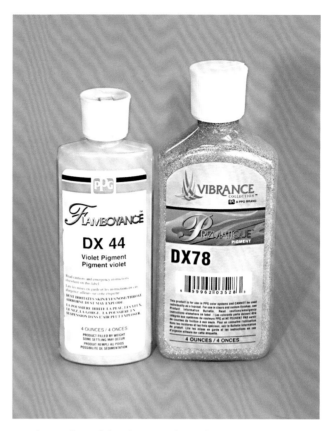

With products like these, each with a unique effect, the sky is the limit for custom paint.

Need help picking your color, or even color combinations? Color cards like these make the job much easier. Each card lists exactly which base and candy color were used to achieve the effect.

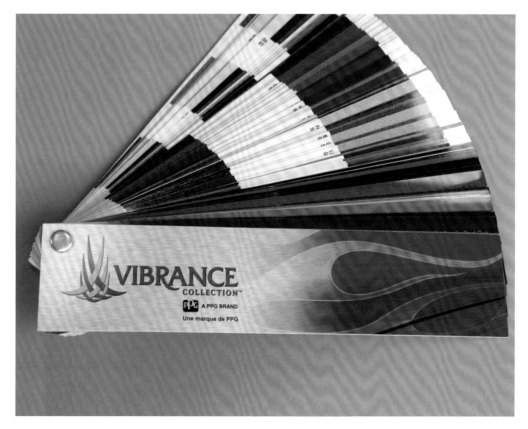

Chapter Three

Spray Guns

Purchase, Adjust and Use

GUN TYPES

Spray guns can be broken down into three types, with variations of course. Most older, traditional guns are siphon type, with the paint cup located under the gun. Air moving through the gun pulls the paint up from the cup where it mixes with the air stream. Though this design makes for a gun with a good feel and good balance, most of these are not HVLP (High Volume Low Pressure) designs.

Spray guns come in all sized and price ranges. The group shown here range from mid-price to premium (left to right). As you spend more money you generally get a better quality gun that will require less input to achieve a certain output.

Gravity feed guns take their name from the fact that gravity is used to feed the paint from the paint cup, which is located above the gun itself, to the air stream. Most new HVLP designs are gravity feed, and with the use of the plastic cup liners there guns can be used in nearly any position, even upside down.

Pressure-feed guns have no paint cup in the conventional sense. Instead, paint under pressure is fed to the gun through a hose. No longer are you limited to one quart of material, which is nice for industrial painting applications.

New Guns

In order to increase the amount of paint that actually hits the surface being painted, and reduce the loss of both paint and solvent to the atmosphere, companies like DeVilbiss, Binks,

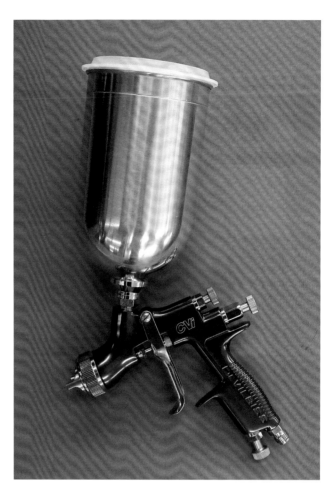

The CVi is a quality, value-priced HVLP gun. Available fluid tips include 1.0, 1.2, 1.3 and 1.4mm.

Sharp and many more began to introduce guns designed to work at a lower pressure. By increasing the volume, while reducing the pressure the designers were able to design guns that would atomize the paint and increase the transfer efficiency enormously.

Though the learning curve was steep for both manufacturers and users, today we have high quality HVLP guns available from a variety of sources that do a great job of both atomizing paint, and meeting all the current regulations, which stipulate no more than 10 psi at the air cap.

While this might all seem like another case of unnecessary regulation, the story has a silver lining for anyone who buys his or her own paint. The increased transfer efficiency means

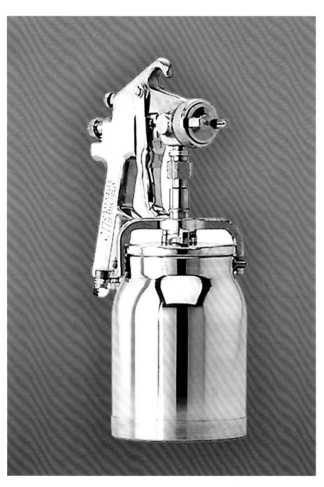

Inexpensive siphon-feed guns are available from a variety of sources. Some are "throw away" guns, no parts are available for repair.

Inside a quality spray gun: here we have a blow up of a new CVi gun.

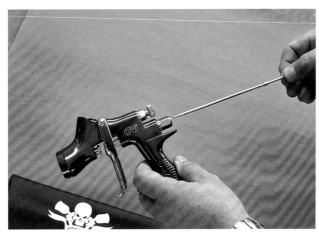

First to be installed, the fluid needle.

Next, John installs the adjustment knob for the needle.

simply that a gallon of paint will cover roughly three times as much surface as it would have twenty or more years ago. Put another way, you need less than half as much paint, and reducer, if you use a good HVLP gun. If you look at the cost of a gallon of high quality paint, you soon realize that the HVLP gun will pay for itself pretty quickly.

The other benefit of HVLP guns is the reduction in overspray and mist in the booth. If more of the paint is actually getting to the motorcycle you're spraying, that means there's less wasted paint in the air. Which means less paint and solvent for you to breathe, or absorb through your skin and mucous membranes – this is especially important in homemade paint booths which seldom have the air movement of a good commercial booth.

How Spray Guns Work

Nearly all current spray guns, whether HVLP or not, operate on the same principle. Essentially, air passing through the spray gun mixes with liquid paint as both exit the gun at the air cap. A two-stage trigger controls both the air and the paint. Pulling the trigger back part way allows air to pass through the gun, while pulling it back farther adds paint to the air already passing through the gun. This feature allows a painter to apply paint across a panel, stop the flow of paint (but leave the air on) at the end of a panel and smoothly resume the flow of paint at the other end of the panel as he starts the next pass.

Paint and air leave the gun at the air cap and immediately begin to mix. Breaking the paint into tiny particles, or atomizing it, occurs in two or three stages, starting at the point where the paint leaves the gun surrounded by a column of air. Additional air leaves the gun from small ports in the air cap. The third stage of atomization is provided by the outboard air ports in the "horns" of the air cap. These ports shape the column of paint into the familiar fan and provide a third level of atomization.

Most guns have two adjustments: air to the

horns which affects the size and shape of the fan, and the material control, which limits the movement of the trigger and thus the needle. In addition, an increasing number of painters put an air-adjusting valve with a pressure gauge on the bottom of the gun where the air hose is connected.

The instructional material that comes with your new gun will include an air pressure recommendation. This recommendation is the right amount of air to feed that gun. Ideally the factory suggested pressure will provide the best pattern. In terms of the care and feeding of your spray gun, the best advice can be summed up in three words: keep it clean.

GUIDELINES AND TIPS

Some people think HVLP – High Volume Low Pressure – means these guns put out a high volume of paint. Yes, they do have great transfer efficiency, but the volume being referred to is the much larger volume of air required to operate the gun.

You need a good compressor to run any air gun, but this is especially true with an HVLP gun. Remember too that an enormous compressor won't do any good unless the connections between the compressor and gun have enough capacity.

This is covered in some detail in Chapter One, but essentially you need airlines in the booth that are at least 3/8 inch ID rather than 5/16 inch. The same applies to the fittings. Most quick couplers have a small ID and tend to limit air delivery to the gun. So pick good connectors and don't put any more hose in the booth than is really needed. The flexible hose should only be as long as necessary to reach all parts of whatever you're painting, to avoid loosing pressure and volume as the air passes through a hose that's way too long.

EQUIPMENT SELECTION

The manufacturers of spray equipment provide a multitude of fluid needle, fluid nozzle and air cap combinations. These combinations are commonly called "gun set-ups." The set-ups are

The fluid tip is next. Each fluid tip is matched to a specific needle. If you change one you have to change the other.

The handy dandy wrench, the one that comes with the gun, is used to tighten the fluid tip.

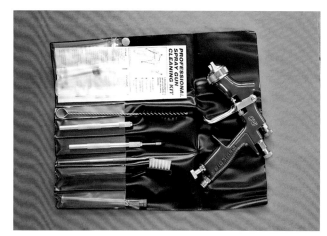

The key to gun longevity is to keep it clean. A kit like this one is available anywhere they sell spray guns.

RTS % Solids Volume	Fluid Ounces/Min.	Fluid Tip Range
1 — 8 %	3 — 5 ounces / min	1.1 — 1.2 mm
9 — 14 %	4 — 6 ounces / min	1.2 — 1.3 mm
15 — 24 %	5 — 8 ounces / min	1.4 — 1.5 mm
25 — 39 %	7 — 9 ounces / min	1.4 — 1.6 mm
40 — 57 %	5 — 7 ounces / min	1.3 — 1.5 mm
60 — 80 %	4 — 6 ounces / min	1.2 — 1.3 mm

A chart like this can be used to determine the initial setup of your new HVLP gun.

generally designed for applying particular categories of refinish material, such as undercoats, basecoats, and clearcoats. It can be difficult to determine the exact gun set up to apply a new product. The best way to understand what kind of performance the different gun set-ups are capable of has to do with a simple ratio: the fluid to air ratio. In other words, the amount of paint coming out of the fluid nozzle vs. the amount of atomizing air being supplied by the air cap. This information can be found on any product information bulletin.

There is also data from gun manufacturers that show how many fluid ounces per minute can be obtained with a particular gun setup. Combining these two pieces of information the chart nearby is a way to choose a gun set up (for an HVLP gravity feed gun) appropriate for the product you are spraying.

In making a selection, keep the following in mind:

A starting point is to choose the tip in the middle of the range.

If you spray wet, choose a tip lower in the range. If you spray dry, choose a tip higher in the range.

These are starting point recommendations only. Your spray technique, size of the panel being sprayed and other variables may affect your choice.

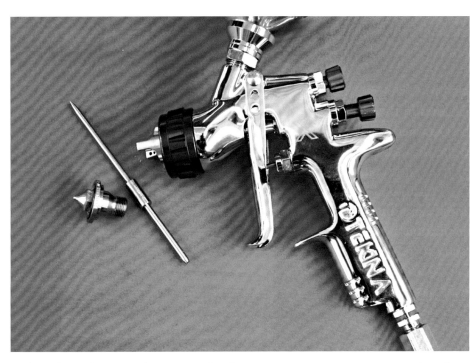

The Tekna, shown with an extra fluid tip set, is a premium spray gun line from DeVilbiss, designed to deliver a great pattern, and with internal components that will not be affected by the new waterborne paint.

PPG performs extensive testing every year with new products and new spray equipment to make specific recommendation for product and gun set ups. You can find these charts in any good technical information book like those provided by PPG.

The reason that the proper gun set up is important is because it can affect the final appearance of the material being applied.

If you have too much fluid and not enough atomizing air, the product can:

•Go on too wet, causing runs, sags, curtains, etc.

•Have too much film build and excess solvent in the film.

•Dry and cure slowly due to excessive film build.

If you have too much atomizing air and not enough fluid, the paint can:

•Go on dry with very little flow, orange peel.

•Have too little film build, not enough paint to perform properly.

•"Flash dry" on the surface and not allow solvents trapped beneath to escape.

•Produce hazing, die-back, or solvent popping.

The balance between paint fluid flow and atomization is too important to be left to chance.

Here you can actually see the difference between three fluid tips, a 1.3, 1.5 and 1.8mm (left to right). These correspond roughly to: clear, color and primer. The needle will have to be changed each time a fluid tip is changed.

As you can see, not all aircaps are the same. Some are designed to spray a particular product, like primer or clear.

Another way to determine the fluid flow of a particular spray gun set up is to perform a "dump test." The result tell you exactly how many fluid ounces per minute can be delivered to the substrate. The following steps explain how to perform the test.

STEP BY STEP DUMP TEST

1. Pour a measured amount (12-20 ounces) of the product you want to apply into your gun cup. The product should already be ready-to-spray (reduced/catalyzed).

2. In a running spray booth or spray area, attach the gun to the compressed air supply and set your air regulator for the correct air pressure.

Adjust spray gun fluid and air controls to full flow.

3. Squeeze the spray trigger fully for 30 seconds. Use a top watch or a wrist watch with a "second" hand/digital display to check timing.

4. Pour the remaining material into a measured (ounce measurements) mixing cup. Note how much fluid is in the mixing cup in ounces. Subtract the amount of fluid left from the starting amount.

5. Multiply the difference from step #4, by 2 (2X 30 seconds = 60 seconds or one minute). This test is a fast way to see how much fluid your gun is actually delivering.

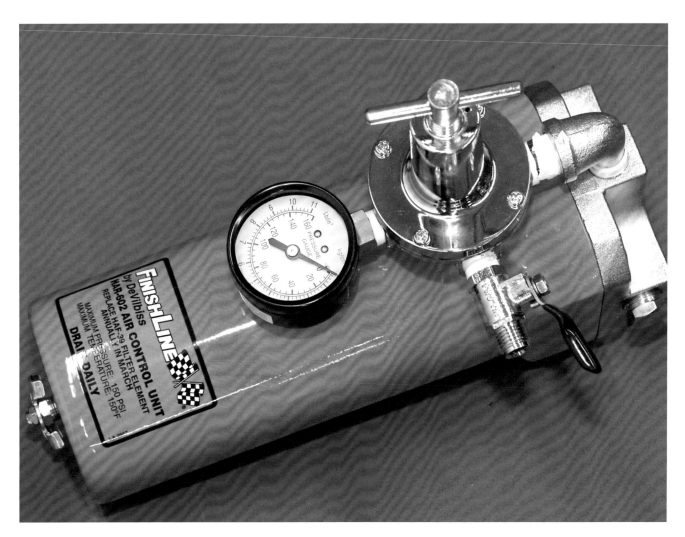

You have to have clean, dry air if you want to do a quality paint job. Removing the water, and even the dirt, isn't enough. Most compressors put a bit of oil in the air, so you need to filter out that oil, which is accomplished by the filter inside this air control unit.

ATOMIZATION

Paint atomization, in the simplest terms, means to beak up a paint liquid into a droplet or spray mist.

•Conventional siphon feed guns atomize paint using high pressure, approximately 35-65 psi at the air cap to burst the paint into a fine spray mist.

•HVLP type spray guns use a high volume of air at low pressure to carry the paint droplet to the painting surface. Air cap pressure for HVLP ranges from 1 – 10 psi.

•Reduced Pressure (RP) or compliant type spray guns combine the characteristics of both conventional and HVLP. The paint is atomized at a high pressure (35 to 65 psi at the cap) but has the transfer efficiency of the HVLP type of spray guns.

Atomization is a critical element that helps determine how any finished automotive paint job will look. Poor atomization will cause a host of problems such as texture or orange peel in colors and clearcoats.

Variables that effect droplet size and atomization include:

•Size of the opening in the fluid tip and air cap.

•Air pressure at the air cap.

•Fluid (paint) delivery system.

Because HVLP spray

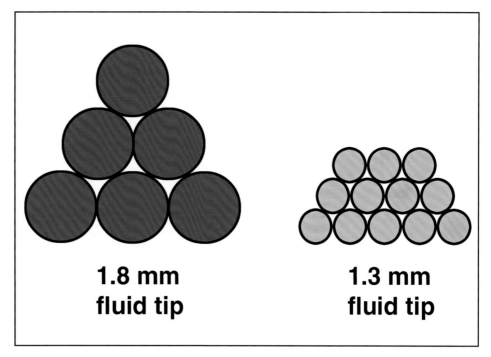

This illustration shows the relative size of the paint particles that come out of two different fluid tips. For good atomization and a nice finish the smaller tip is the way to go.

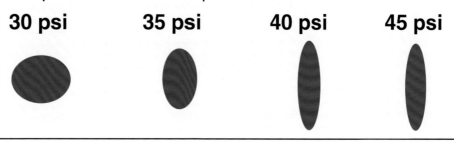

In this example, the optimum pressure will be 40 psi (HVLP air cap pressure must not be >10psi).

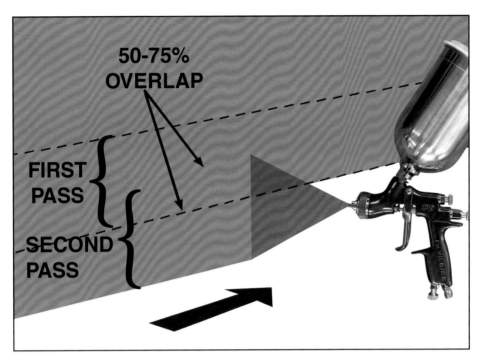

Most paints call for a 50% overlap between passes, with some custom paints, like candies, the manufacturer may call for as much as 75%.

uneven film. Applying an even film is very important to obtaining proper film build and drying characteristics. The proper gun angle also reduces the possibility of striping or mottling when applying metallics.

SPRAY GUN SPEED, PATH AND OVERLAP

Spray gun travel speed should be such as to ensure uniform film build. The best way to judge gun speed is to really look at the way the paint is striking the panel. Ask yourself the following questions while applying refinish products:

- Is the paint product laying down correctly?
- Is it wet enough?
- Is it even enough?

The spray gun path or "overlap" should provide the proper "wetness" without creating excessive film build. Using a 50% (minimum) – 75% (maximum) overlap is the best "path" to take for even film build characteristics. Increasing the overlap gives better metallic control and improves clearcoat film build. The diagram shows appropriate angle, path and overlap when applying refinish products.

GUN DISTANCE

The distance from the surface will vary somewhat with the size and type of repair and the spray equipment. The recommended distance for most PPG products is 6 to 9 inches.

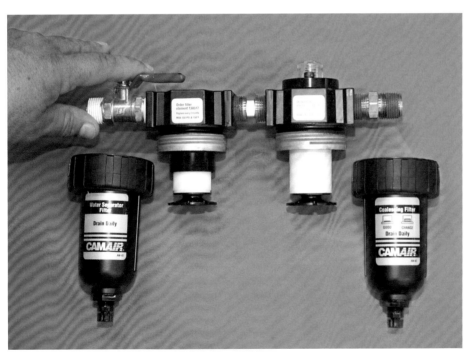

This relatively inexpensive two-stage filter unit will remove water, as well as dirt and also, oil in the airline. Small finger-tight valves on the bottom of each canister make it easy to eliminate any moisture that accumulates.

Holding the gun closer than recommend restricts the separation of atomized particles resulting in excessive wetting of the products.

The technique does several things:

•Pounds solvent-rich material on the surface which provides insufficient film build.

•Slows dry and cure times.

•Traps solvents that can lead to die back and solvent popping.

Holding the gun back from the surface farther than recommended allows the atomized product to widely separate and will lack the required wetting on impact.

This technique does several things:

•Too much material lost with in-flight solvent loss

•Dries too fast (will have a dry, rough film).

•Insufficient film build.

•Improper wetting of material.

•May require more coats to cover.

Holding the gun at the recommended distance (6 to 9 inches) allows the proper amount of material to reach the panel and flow out.

The technique does several things:

•Allows the correct in-flight solvent loss.

•Dries and cures correctly.

•Provides even film build.
•Allows for proper adhesion.

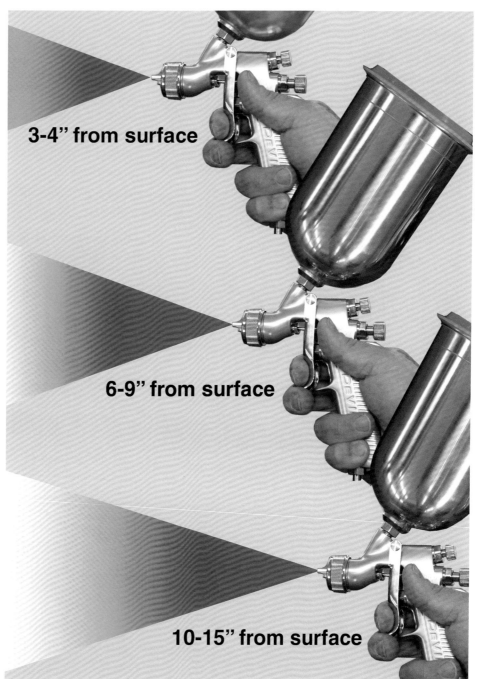

3-4" from surface

6-9" from surface

10-15" from surface

Be sure to follow the manufacturer's recommendation regarding the gun-to-surface distance. The distance obviously affects the width of the fan, but also determines how wet or dry the paint film will be.

Gun Adjustment & Air Pressure

A great deal can be learned by taking the time to do a simple pattern test. Instead of just spraying a pattern on a piece of paper, it's more instructive to turn the aircap 90 degrees, and then intentionally apply too much paint. Apply enough paint that it starts to run. Now you can really see where the bulk of the paint is being applied. And if you look at the edge you can gauge the droplet size as well.

Too much air pressure will give you a split pattern, but that doesn't mean you want to turn the pressure way down. More pressure will provide better atomization and overall performance.

Think of an engine, do you want to choke an engine and run it at less than 100% efficiency? Each gun comes with a recommendation for air pressure. Too many painters are running their guns at 10 psi (at the gun) when the recommended air pressure is 15 psi.

With HVLP you only have 10 psi at the cap, not 65 psi to break up the big droplets. You have to use a smaller fluid tip to create a smaller droplet. You can restrict the needle trigger pull to create a smaller droplet, but the needle may not be centered when it isn't pulled all the way back. So it's better to have the needle all the way back and use a smaller fluid tip.

This image and the one below illustrate the effect that additional air pressure has on the size...

...of the droplets that leave the gun. Same gun, same fluid tip, the only difference is the air pressure...

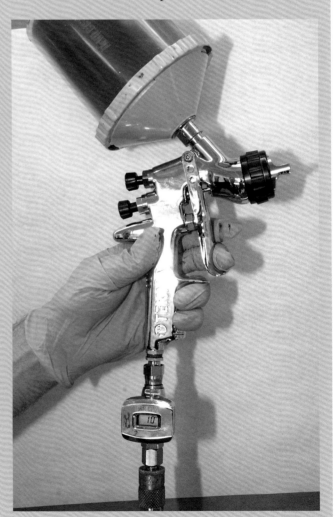

...which is why it's important to know what the pressure is at the gun.

Gun Adjustment

The start of the test, first you have follow the recommendations for gun-to-surface distance.

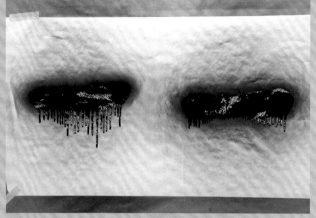

How much is too much air pressure? When the pattern starts to split as we see on the right.

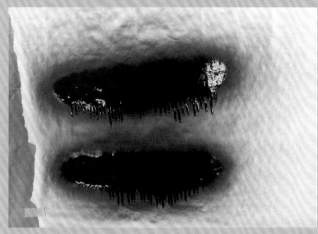

The first pull, with a full trigger pull, an open fan, and a little too much air pressure.

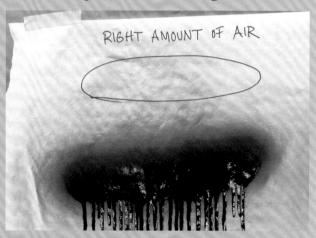

Here's a good pattern that also exhibits good atomization.

As we turn down the pressure we get a better pattern, like the one on the right.

Once we have things dialed in, we do a standard pattern without applying too much paint.

Chapter Four

Metal Preparation

Getting Down to the Bare Facts

Most Custom bike projects start out as bare metal. The frame and tins usually come without any primer on them. So we will deal with bare metal in this chapter.

First we must realize that bare metal will start to rust in 30 minutes at 50% humidity, even if the rust is not visible. One way to deal with this is to use a metal cleaner and conditioner on the bare metal before applying any primer. PPG makes DX 579 metal cleaner and DX 520

When it comes to bare steel, you need to get it coated with something right away, as rust waits for no man.

The 520 product is a metal conditioner that leaves a zink-type, rust inhibiting coating behind.

metal conditioner for this purpose. DX 579 is a strong cleaner that cleans and neutralizes any rust. It also leaves a phosphate coating that looks like rust which will protect the metal. DX 520 follows the DX 579 to further protect the metal from rusting and leaves a zinc type coating which is a light grey color. This zinc-type coating is much easier to prime over than the phosphate coating. This is a wet process, the products are applied wet and rinsed off with water. The DX 579 leaves a phosphate coating on the metal immediately so the water rinse is not touching the metal. The DX 579 and 520 must be kept wet for 3-5minutes and not allowed to dry before being rinsed off. Once the metal is cleaned and dried it is rust free and protected from any surface rust. It must, however, be primed within eight hours. DPLF 40 epoxy primer with DPLF 401 catalyst is the best

choice for a primer. This system duplicates the same process new cars go through to protect them from rusting. There are some draw backs to this system, as this process is for smooth metal. Anything that has been sandblasted or ground with a grinder leaves too rough of a surface for the phosphate and zinc coatings. If any body filler is present the cleaners can't be used, instead the body filler should go over the epoxy primer after it has dried for three days.

The next best way to deal with bare metal is to sand with 80 to 180 grit sand paper either by hand or with a sander. Wipe it down with acetone and prime with DPLF epoxy primer with DPLF 401 catalyst immediately, keeping in mind what we said earlier: bare metal will start to rust in 30 minutes at 50% humidity. If you are applying body filler, do that first, then sand down the rest of the metal, wipe with acetone,

Once the metal is bare, you want to wipe it down with DX 579 as soon as possible. 579 will clean the metal and retard any flash rust.

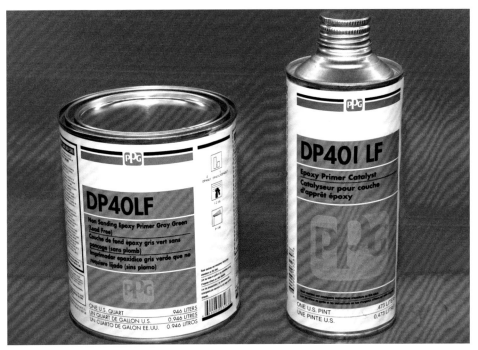

This two-part primer provides tenacious bonding to bare metal and gives great corrosion protection. The next step would likely be a primer-surfacer.

then prime. Acetone is a good choice because it evaporates very quickly and won't soak into the pores of the metal or body filler like other solvent based cleaners will. Do not use a water-based cleaner over bare metal or body filler.

SANDBLASTING

Sandblasting cleans and abrades the metal surface, but is difficult to clean if it gets dirty before priming. Sandblasted parts should be blown off with clean dry air and primed immediately. Again DPLF Epoxy primmer with DPLF 401 catalyst will provide the best corrosion protection.

Bare Metal should always be primed with a primer that provides corrosion protection first, then a primer-surfacer can be applied for sanding, followed by a primer-sealer to fill 320 – 400 grit scratches and provide a uniform surface/color from sand-throughs, before applying color.

PPG's DPLF epoxy primer mixed with DPLF 401, provides the best corrosion protection and adhesion when applied over bare metal or PPG's metal cleaner DX 579 and conditioner DX 520. Etch primers like DX 1791, or DX 170, provide good adhesion and some corrosion protection but can not be used over sandblasted metal or metal cleaned with DX 579 / DX 520. Etch primers should not be used over body filler. Etch

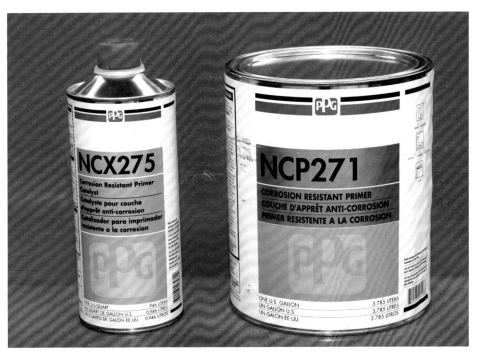

NCP 271 can be mixed either as a standard primer surfacer, or as a high-build primer to better fill scratches and small imperfections.

primers work best over new clean metal that does not need to be sanded.

Once bare metal is clean, the rust is neutralized, and the metal is primed to provide adhesion and corrosion protection. The next step is to smooth out the tins or frame. If bodywork was done before the primer was applied, a primer-surfacer is sprayed, which can be sanded smooth. PPG makes primer-surfacers that can be mixed as high-build surfacers or standard primer-surfacers. Some of these products include: K36, K38, DPS 3055, NCP250, NCP 271, and NCP 280. No matter which one you use be sure to follow the instructions for mixing and dry times between coats. Primer-surfacers shrink when the proper flash times between coats (5 – 10 minutes) are ignored. Avoid excessive coats of primer. Body filler and glaze products are made for this. They dry much quicker than primer and cost less.

Sanding a primer-surfacer should start with 180 - 220 grit sand paper. Use a guide coat which is a light coat of a darker or lighter color sprayed over the primer-surfacer (guide coats are illustrated farther along in the hands-on chapters). The guide coat will show the low areas or sand scratches that need to be addressed as you sand. Try to sand with a block and not your bare hands, especially on the sheet metal so you don't sand

With a Deltron label, this DPS 3055 is another of the modern products that can be mixed and used in more than one way, as either a primer surfacer or high-build primer.

All the good fillers are two part products, consisting of the filler itself and the hardener. Note the plastic pallet, no cardboard.

The hardener should be kneaded before being used. Always note the expiration date.

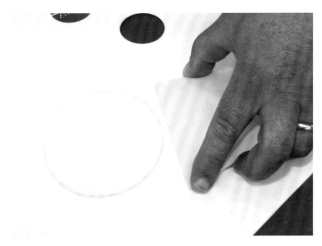

With the Rage product they recommend a four inch puddle - as measured by a four inch squeegee.

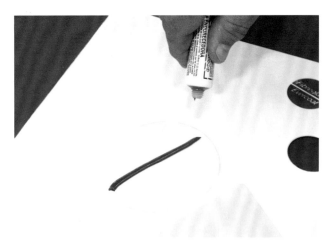

To get the correct ratio of filler to hardener, run one strip of hardener as shown across the four inch puddle.

groves into the parts from the pressure of your palms and fingers. Once you have blocked out the parts with 180 – 220 grit, take time to inspect the parts. If there are low areas, pin holes or deep scratches, mix up some glaze with white cream hardener and fill those low areas. Then sand the areas with 180 grit sandpaper. If the area is larger then a dime you will need to spray two more coats of primer surfacer on that area. If there are a lot of bare metal spots and a lot of glaze coat, then spray two to three more coats of primer surfacer on the whole part. If they're small pin holes or scratches, you used a white cream hardener, if and you don't have any metal showing yet, you can finish sanding with 320 – 400 grit sandpaper after re-guide coating. Once you've sanded with 320-400 grit sand paper you can spray a coat of primer-sealer to fill the 320-400 scratches and cover any small sand-throughs.

If you do not want to spray a primer-sealer, finish sand with 600 grit sand paper and be sure you haven't sanded through to any bare metal or body filler.

Spraying a primer-sealer insures good adhesion to any sand-throughs and provides a uniform color and surface to spray your color over. Not all sealers PPG makes will be the best ones for painting motorcycle parts. K36 and DAS 3021, DAS 3025 and DAS 3027 are great sealers. K36 can be tinted and the DAS sealers come in white, grey and dark grey colors. These sealers may be too fast when the temperatures get hot and you are trying to spray lots of parts and a frame. These sealers are designed to spray base coat over in as little as 5 minutes, if 30 minutes go by at warmer temperatures these sealers can wrinkle when you spray base over them. If you can not spray over them quickly, they should dry for a couple of hours before painting over them. DPLF mixed with DPLF402 makes a better sealer for these parts giving you plenty of time to spray everything. DPLF comes in white, black, green, blue, red oxide and grey.

BODY FILLERS

Body fillers are an important part to molding that custom frame and finishing off the custom extensions welded to the tank. Body fillers are not a substitute for poor metal work so they should be kept to a minimum. When a lot of filler is needed or you are filling an area that was welded, an all-metal type filler is a better choice. This product works the same as body filler but has aluminum mixed with the resin. Another good choice is a fiberglass filler that uses fiberglass mixed with the resin. These fillers are stronger then regular body fillers, but do not sand as easily. Body fillers can be applied over these fillers to finish off your work.

Body fillers should be applied over clean, not rusty, metal that has been ground with 36 - 40 grit to get good adhesion. They can also be applied over PPG's DPLF epoxy primer mixed with DPLF401 that has dried three days for the best results. Though the instructions are sometimes confusing, be sure to mix the body filler properly. When you've mixed enough of it to figure out the right consistency, use the color of your favorite mix to judge the mixture. That color will give you consistent mixing every time. Just be sure you get the same color cream hardener every time. Too much cream hardener can still cause bleeding problems later and the filler will dry too fast giving poor adhesion to the metal. If you use too little cream hardener the filler will not fully dry. There's a reason a gallon of filler comes with one tube of cream hardener, if you're using more (or less) then that you're mixing it wrong. Inconsistent mixing will cause spots that are softer than the surrounding area, resulting in shrinkage problems under your paint job. Try to avoid body filler on oil tanks.....these get really hot in traffic and the heat can cause the filler to blister.

Mix your body filler with a putty knife on a flat, smooth surface. Automotive door glass, plexiglas, or a similar surface works very well. Any automotive paint store will have the proper tools for sale. The body filler should not be shak-

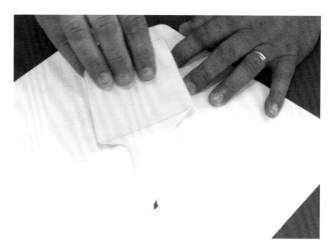

To mix the material, fold the filler over on itself, trying not to get the hardener on the squeegee.

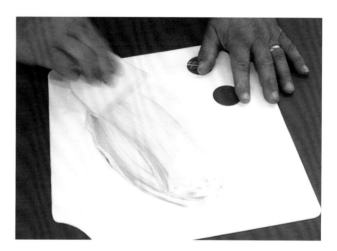

Then mix the material further by pulling through the mix with downward pressure.

When it's fully mixed the material has a uniform color. A thin layer will extend the work time.

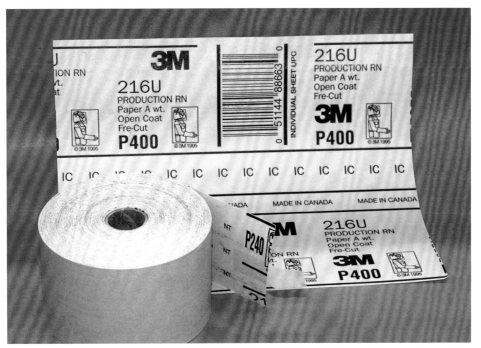

Sand paper comes in a wide array of grits and formats. The new designations, preceded by a P, are not exactly the same as the old grit numbers.

The range of available grits includes some very fine papers useful for finishing.

en on a paint shaker or whipped in the can with a blending action, this will cause air bubbles and pin holes. When mixing the body filler with the cream hardener use the putty knife to scrape the filler off the mixing board, turning it over and over and pressing down each time. The process is like kneading bread, as if you know how to do that! The idea is to mix it while pushing out the air pockets. Do not stir it as this whips air into the filler. As we explained, air bubbles will create pin holes later. When spreading the filler use a good plastic spreader to push the first coat down into your surface. Sanding the body filler you can start with a cheese grater (surform blade) for large fills. This tool is handy for shaping. Next, block sand with 36 - 40 grit sand paper stopping just before the area is level, finish off with 80 grit sand paper. With practice you should be able to apply enough body filler the first time so that multiple applications are not needed. This is where trouble begins when the different applications are not consistent. A coat of glaze should be used to finish off the filler. This lighter material will flow into pin holes and fill scratches left by the coarse sand paper. Buy glaze that comes with white cream hardener because this prevents bleeding. Sand the glaze coat with 120 - 180 grit sandpaper. You are now ready for primer-surfacer.

Body Fillers can go over: DPLF epoxy primers, sandblasted metal, ground metal 36 – 80 grit grinder discs. Body fillers can not go over: Etch primers DX 1791, DX 170, metal cleaner DX 579, metal conditioner DX 520.

STRIPING...

..that got your attention! Not all Custom Cycle projects will start with bare metal parts. Some new parts will come already primed. If it's a Harley-Davidson part it will come with PPG E-Coat Primer on it. Any time you get a part that's been primed, test it by soaking a rag with lacquer thinner and placing it on the primer. After a few minutes check to see if the primer wipes off. If it does it's a thermoplastic resin and you don't want to paint over it. Wipe it all off, sand it off or sandblast it. Once it's bare metal treat it accordingly (note the information that follows in this chapter). If the primer does not wipe off it's a thermo set primer, good stuff! Leave it on. Sand it with 320 - 400 grit paper or scuff it with a red 3M type scuff pad seal it and paint it. If you are doing body work, welding on it etc, grind that area with 40 - 80 grit, feather back the primer with 180 - 220 grit and sand the rest with 320 - 400 grit. Prime bare metal with a primer, then use a primer-surfacer.

If you are painting over a new factory paint job like

Big sheets like this can be cut and wrapped around a flexible pad for block sanding.

Unlike a conventional sander, a DA can sand a surface and take off paint without the typical gouging and swirl patterns...

...the key is in this hub, which separates the disc from the motor. The net result is a sanding disc that vibrates as much as it rotates. With this model the hub can be locked so the DA becomes a conventional sander. Mississippi Welders Supply Co.

that on a Harley-Davidson, do a solvent test first to be sure the paint doesn't wipe off or soften. If it doesn't, sand with 320 - 400 grit, spray it with sealer and then apply a topcoat. If there are logos or stripes, or it's a custom paint job, be sure to strip the old paint off! If you have access to an electronic mil gauge use that to determine how thick the paint is. If there are more than 13 mils of paint you have to take it off. You can use a chemical paint stripper, but it's a mess. Sand blasting is another option, but you have to be sure the operator knows how to blast sheet metal, otherwise the blasting creates too much heat and the metal will warp. A better blasting option is to media blast with a plastic media. This works better than sand basting and creates minimal heat. You can also try good old sanding, use 80 grit on an air sander. Don't use a DA, that would take too long.

SANDING TIPS AND GRITS

Sanding can be performed wet or dry. Bare metal should never be wet sanded. Rust! Primer-surfacers can be sanded wet or dry. I prefer dry. If you sand through primer-surfacer while wet sanding the metal underneath will get wet. Rust!

SANDING METAL

80 grit to 120 grit leaves a better surface.

Stick-on discs in all the common grits are available for a DA, which makes it really easy to just rip one off, stick on another and get back to work.

Don't use coarse grits 24, 36, 40 or 60 unless you are putting body filler over it. More grinder marks mean more coats of primer surfacer and more hand sanding.

SANDING BODY FILLER

Start with 40 grit and finish with 80 - 120 grit. This will leave smaller scratches for the primer surfacer to fill and less shrinkage.

GLAZE COAT

Start with 180 grit finish with 220 - 320 grit

PRIMER SURFACER

Start with 180 - 220 grit finish with 320 – 400 grit. If you want to spray base coat over a sanded primer surface finish with 600 grit sand paper. Do not spray black base coat over a sanded primer surface, always spray black over a sealer.

PRIMER SEALER

If you need to sand, use 600 - 800 grit. Use DX 330 wax and grease remover as a lubricant for fresh paint that has dried 30-90 minutes. Let DX 330 dry before painting.

BASE COAT

To de nib DBC base coat or DBC 500 use 600-800 grit. Use DX 330 wax and grease remover as a lubricant. Let dry before spraying more paint.

Big grinder/sanders, like this seven inch air-powered model, are better left for true grinding operations. Powerful tools like this can score the metal and add a great deal of heat - essentially doing more harm than good.

The Hookit system is designed to "snap" right onto the sanding pad on your small grinder or DA.

Chapter Five

Design & Art Work

From Concept to Masking

How do you come up with great custom paint ideas? Attend as many bike shows and events as you can, take a lot of pictures of the paint jobs, not the girls. This should help to get you inspired. But don't become a copy cat. The last thing you want to do is copy another custom painter's design. So try looking elsewhere for some inspiration. Look at race cars, from NASCAR to drag racing to everything in between. Don't forget boats, from off shore to pleasure and drag boats. You can get lots of different graphic ideas and see lots of great use of colors. Try the magazine rack at

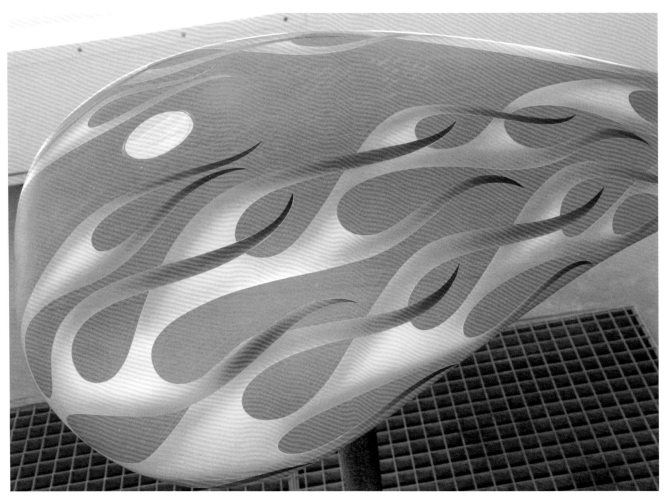

When it comes to a really nice set of flames, some artists start with a sketch while others, like Dave Perewitz, just start with a roll of 1/8 inch tape and do the "sketch" right on the tank.

your local Barnes & Noble. Magazines are full of ads designed by graphic designers, you will be amazed at the use of colors and the art work in these ads. Check out the sunset and sunrise shots in the travel magazines, note the blue water and the colors of the tropical fish. Mother-nature does a pretty good job of putting colors together.

OK, now you've got some ideas running around in your head. Some custom painters can go up to tank with a roll of 1/8 inch masking tape, and in a matter of minutes a wild design appears. If you're not that lucky, try some sketches first. What, you can't draw? That's OK. Take a picture of the whole bike, get a good side view. If the gas tank has a dash or emblems that go on you'll need to know where they go. Also, where is the filler located? Now take the pictures and blow them up on a copier to an 11x17 inch size. Next, get some tracing paper and sit down and trace the bike. Don't worry about all the details, just get a good outline. Now run off a bunch of copies and start sketching your ideas. During this process you may come up with some new designs you hadn't thought of. If you're going for some type of a two-tone paint with a graphic to split the colors, try to tie in all the stripes so the whole job flows. You don't want it to look like you've added bags, or a fairing, after the fact. This may take awhile, be patient.

This is the very beginning of the art work seen in Chapter Seven, nothing more than a series of tape lines stretched across the tank. The good news - if you don't like part of the design, all you have to do is pull the tape and start over.

The finished tapeout. Now is the time to really analyze the design. Stand back and give it a good look, or wait until tomorrow to see if you really like it, because this is the last chance to change the layout.

A good example of a flame job that is well balanced, and fits the bike as well. Note the way the flames on the front fender wrap all the way around the tire.

Try to keep some balance in your design. For example, don't load the top of the tank with lots of graphics and then have nothing on the sides. If you're doing a flame job, then flame the rear fender along with the front fender and gas tank. If you want flames, that may be a little tougher to draw out at first. Practice, practice, practice. Your sketches may just be rough ideas to help you lay out your design, and it's a good way to put colors together. This will give you some direction so you don't get started on the tank and can't figure out how to tie in the bags or front fender. If all else fails there are artists out there who will do the design work for you.

Remember, good bike design shows movement. Good design will not grow old over time, and a simpler design stands the test of time. Try to ensure that your design flows with the lines of the bike.

CHOOSING COLORS

Dark colors will make the bike look smaller. Chrome will stand out better against dark colors, graphics or flames will jump out next to a dark color. Lighter colors will make the bike look bigger and the chrome doesn't pop as much. Bright colors will make the bike pop in a crowd where dark colors tend to blend in. Remember those drawings you did? Once you come up with a design you like, make multiple copies and start coloring. This will help

This very special "soft tail" uses a paint job based on PPG Bright&Bold, with Keith Hanson graphics that follow the lines and contours of the sheet metal to enhance the overall shape.

you put colors together that work. Again, look at pictures in the magazines of things you like and pay attention to the different colors and how they work together.

There are cool colors to choose from, greens, blues and purples. These work well together. You could also choose warm colors like yellow, red and orange that work well together. The trick is putting the cool and warm colors together. You can get a color wheel from an art store, and books on color that will help you to understand how color theory works. The primary colors; blue, yellow, and red, have different shades in automotive paint. There are green-shade blues and red-shade blues. There are blue-shade reds and yellow-shade reds, red-shade yellows, and green-shade yellows. Then there are the secondary colors. Greens between yellow and blues that range from yellow greens like lime green, to green, to blue-shade greens like teal. The purples range from blue-shade reds, to purple, magenta and hot pink. Then oranges that range from red-shade yellow red/orange, to orange, to school-bus yellow.

PPG has tint charts with color wheels on them that will help you to see these different colors. A green usually dose not look good with a red because they are opposite colors on a color wheel. To make red and green work together use a yellow-shade green (lime green), and a blue-shade red

Blues, purples and magentas create a bold splash of color on the tank and fender of this Perewitz custom. Sometimes the only way to tell if two colors go together is to do a test panel.

In someways this design is similar to the one above. Keith Hanson created a long tapered panel on the tank and filled it with colors that work with the PPG "O So Orange."

There are various ways to make a template. Here I placed the paper over the layout, and then traced the edges with a pencil.

(purple or magenta). Try a green shade yellow with a green shade blue, or a red shade yellow with a red shade blue.

An accent or pinstripe color can be subtle and blend in, or be contrasting and bold. An example would be a yellow-orange fade paint job over a red-shade candy blue (cobalt). The pinstripe could be a blue that would be subtle and blend with the cobalt blue color, or a red that would blend with the yellow orange flames. A good example of a contrasting color would be a yellow-shade green (lime green) that would make the flames pop off the blue back ground.

With all the color theory and rules, sometimes the best thing is to get out your copies and start coloring. Felt tip markers work best, because they resemble candy paint colors. Try different combinations until you get the one that knocks your socks off. If you come up with a few different combinations you like, hang them up on the beer refrigerator for a week and see which one stands out the most. Some times the one you thought was best will not be your first choice after looking at it over and over again.

THE LAYOUT

There are many different types and sizes of tape available. We stick with 3M because they make a great product that is consistent and designed to work with automotive paints. Be careful choosing tape based on price. Tape must stick, yet

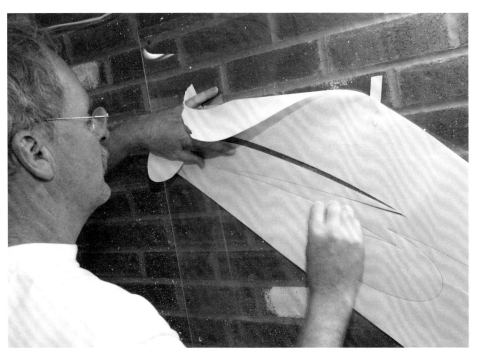

Next, I cut out the design with a razor blade on a piece of plexiglass mounted to the wall.

come off easily when the job is done. The tape must be able to bend in a tight radius and stick once you put it down. Do not get tape wet and avoid the hot sun.

There are paper, plastic and vinyl tapes that are used for specific jobs. Anytime a stripe or flame is going to be pinstriped a paper tape like 3M crepe tape (green or beige color) works very well. When spraying light applications of basecoats these tapes will leave clean edges. This 3M paper tape comes in sizes ranging from 1/8 to 1/2 inch for laying out flames and graphics. The same tape comes in widths from 1/2 inch to two inches which work great for bigger areas.

Once I have the template positioned carefully, I can mark out the design with chalk.

When doing ghost flames or tape shading where no pin stripes will follow, a vinyl or plastic tape will do the trick like 3M's green fine line or blue plastic tape. This tape comes in various widths, including 1/8 and 1/4 inch widths. The green fine line tape also comes in 1/16 inch for tight curves and smaller flames. These tapes work well over fresh basecoat without leaving tape marks. Don't pull hard and stretch this tape when doing lay outs or it won't stick.

The blue plastic tape works great for beginners when laying out flames because it can be lifted off and put back down several times without affecting the adhesion. This tape works best if you are laying out a stripe, or flames, over a finished paint job and do not want to re clear the whole

And then it's just a matter of taping out the identical design on the second bag.

What we call tape is actually a wide range of products that include the traditional masking tape, as well as the plastic tape.

job. Once you have masked the stripe or flames you can use a 3M fine scuff pad to sand the paint for adhesion. The blue plastic tape holds up to the scuff pad real well where the other tapes won't.

Laying out flames and tight corners are best done using the 1/8 inch tape. The 1/4 inch tape is used for laying out longer, flowing-type graphics. The wider the tape the easier it is to keep straight lines and smooth flowing arcs.

When laying out flames and graphics remember the flame or graphic looks bigger then it is. The flame is going to be the inside of the tape, but as you lay it out you're focusing on the outside edge of the tape so you think the flame is 1/8 inch bigger than it really is. This is also why, as you begin, it is a good idea to draw out your flames or graphics on the tank. You can use a piece of good old fashioned school chalk. White works best except on white of course. The excess chalk wipes off easily and doesn't react with the paint. There are Stabilo pencils that sign painters use that also work really well. Stabilo pencils wipe off with water. Stabilos do not react with the paint, but the lines are hard to wipe off a sanded surface so be careful. The surface will appear clean until you spray the clear coat. Some painters just use a #2 pencil.

A great flame job that flows may not be exactly the same from side to side, trust your eyes and let it go. Graphics can be duplicated

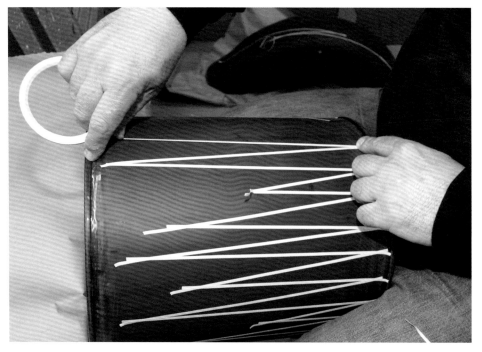

A can like this can make good demonstration project, or even a good way to test a new color or layout. Here we start the layout with 1/8 inch masking tape.

66

with exactness from side to side by cutting a paper template so you can be sure both spaces match. You can make a pattern with a pounce wheel like we did in Chapter Seven. Pounce wheels, chalk pads, and fine artist chalk made for this can be bought from any good art store. Carpenters' chalk from a builders supply stores will work also. Just pour it in an old stinky sock.

When working with patterns, be sure to tape the paper down real well or have someone hold it in place so it doesn't move around on you when you are making the pattern and chalking it on the other side. Patterns work great on tank tops and flat bags, but are tricky on curved surfaces.

The next step in this case is to use one inch wide tape, which is laid down so it covers half the 1/8 inch tape.

MASKING

Masking off your flames or graphics can be done many different ways. Good old fashioned masking tape works the best. Several different sizes work well, use two inch tape for the bigger areas and thinner tapes to fill in the narrow spots. Masking should be neat and as flat as possible. Bad masking can trap dirt, and cause overspray to get through into unwanted areas. To finish the masking, start by going around the flames or graphics with 1/4 inch paper tape. Keep it on top of the 1/8 inch tape that you used to lay out the design. This creates a double layer and wider area. Now, when it is time to

An X-acto knife or razor blade is used to trim the masking tape. Make sure the blade is sharp, and only cut through one layer of tape, not into the paint.

Always pull the wide masking tape first. If you are careful in the way it way laid down, it will come off in big sections. Next, pull the 1/8 inch tape.

unmask, all tape will be on top of this 1/4 inch tape. You just grab the edge of this row of tape and pull everything up in one layer. This works especially well with flames.

Next, run your 2 inch tape over the 1/4 inch and trim it with a razor blade. If you trim as you go, a piece of tape at a time, you won't have over-lapping layers that require more pressure to cut through - which can result in cut marks on the paint. Start masking on one side and work your way across. This will prevent missed areas, and all the tape will pull off in one pull because each piece you put down overlaps the first. Once you're done, run your finger along all the edges of the flame or graphic, checking for any over, or under, masked or missed areas. If you are masking large areas with paper don't use newspaper or cheap stuff, paint can bleed through and cause damage.

The 3M white masking paper is good, 3M also makes a gold coated paper that is waterproof and solvent proof. Other ways to mask are to use rolls of sticky paper called transfer paper that the sign industry uses. Transfer paper lends itself to air-brushing because you are spraying less paint over it. Transfer papers are great for cut-out designs, but if you are cutting over base coat the cut marks will show. You have to be careful or pinstripe that edge.

The white transfer papers will bleed if you are not careful. The overspray gets fuzzy on top and the more paint you are spraying the worse it becomes, and you end up with a lot of dirt in your paint. There are clear transfer papers that are more solvent resistant, but dried paint doesn't stick to them. So if you are spraying multiple coats with dry times in between, you can get chunks of paint

Here's the job before the clearcoat or any pinstripes. Note the clean edges, you really don't need pinstripes on this layout.

blowing off into your wet paint.

Vinyl paint-mask from a sign shop works well. Be sure it is paint mask and not vinyl or banner material, or it may not come off when you're done painting. You can also buy a product called spray mask. Also from the sign industry, this is like spraying down a clear rubber coating. It works really well on curved surfaces and is clear. The trouble is it takes a long time to dry and you have to cut and peel out areas you want to paint.

It's always best to wait until the paint is fully dry before unmasking. That means all the solvent has evaporated. It you try to unmask paint that is dry on top and wet underneath (because you used a fast evaporating solvent), it is a pretty safe bet the paint will peel as you unmask. Paint that is wet with solvent under a dry surface has zero adhesion at this stage. You need to wait. A slower solvent will let you unmask sooner. You can always try while the paint is still wet, the danger is if any tape or a paint edge falls into the wet paint, you're screwed. If it is a big job with lots of flames it will start to dry before you're finished unmasking and you'll get some peeling. Just wait!

When you unmask it's a good idea to leave the first tape you put down for the lay out. Grab that second layer of 1/4 inch paper tape you put down and start where you started the first

Here we're pulling the tape off the tank seen in Chapter Seven. The wide masking tape comes off first, the skinny tape is next. Always pull the 1/8 inch tape away from itself so it is less likely to pull any paint.

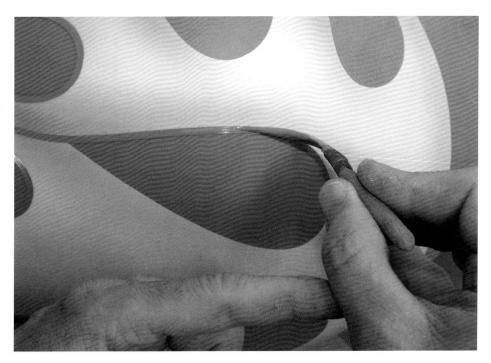

Pinstripes are more than a way to cover the edge between the graphic and the main paint job. Pinstripes are a major graphic component of their own. You can pick a color that blends or one that contrasts with the rest of the design.

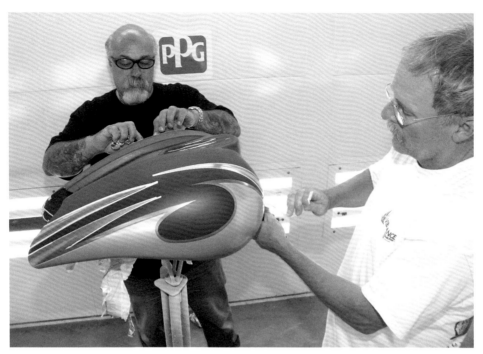

time. It should all pull up in on nice piece. Now when you pull up the 1/8 inch tape, pull it straight back against itself. It will trim the edge of the paint and leave a clean edge. You can also watch the edge as you're pulling without the other masking getting in the way. If an edge stars to come up stop, push it down and let it dry more before pulling the tape.

To prevent tape marks over base coats. First, use slower solvent in the basecoat so that when it dries, it is dry all the way through. Always spray a coat if DBC 500 clear over your last coat of color before taping. The DBC 500 is an intercoat/mid-coat of basecoat clear that should also be reduced with a slower solvent. Let it dry before taping. If tape marking occurs, the tape marks in the clear will not show when the top coat of clear is applied. The DBC 500 prevents the metallic or pearl underneath from being marked by the tape.

Another Bagger tank, seen farther along in the book, is unmasked. Sometimes a slow reducer will get the job done sooner rather than later, as the slower reducer will allow the paint to dry-through faster.

There are a few common-sense rules to tape and taping:

Don't leave tape or a masked off flame job in the sun. Store tape in a cool area. Don't get tape or masking wet with water. Don't lay tape down on a dirty surface. The dirt sticks to the edge of the tape and then stays on the tank when you use that dirty roll of tape later. Finally, don't stretch fine line and plastic tapes when laying out flames and graphics.

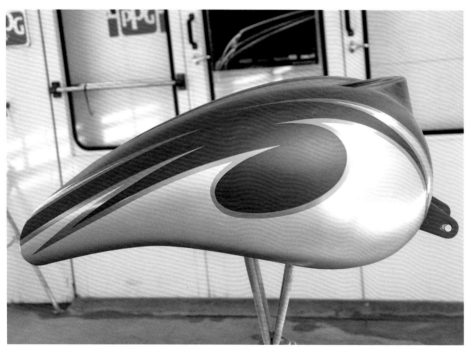

Here's the tank, after the tape is pulled, before the pinstripes or clearcoat. Again, the edges are pretty clean and crisp because of the care we took in laying down the tape.

Q&A Paul Stoll, PPG Trainer

Paul, how about some background on you, how did you end up as a trainer for PPG?

I grew up in Southern California, going to drag races and cars shows. I took body and paint classes in tech school and the teacher showed us a lot of tricks. After high school I painted full time, worked in a restoration shop, did a bunch of magazine work. I eventually moved to Boise, Idaho, where I worked for myself for awhile doing restoration and paint work. Eventually I became a jobber and paint distributor in Boise, and I often took my customers to the PPG training center. After a number of years the trainer there offered me a job. I turned him down three times. Then they stated a custom paint program, so I said, "yes, if I can I develop the custom paint program and teach the classes."

When I go to paint a motorcycle what are my basic options in terms of types of paint? Are all of what we call custom paints a urethane?

All are acrylic urethanes, lacquers have gone by the wayside.

Urethanes are faster, which means you can tape on them faster. Lacquer would tape-mark bad. Urethanes are more durable, they won't crack and check like the old lacquer jobs. The biggest

advantage is you can do the same job with fewer coats, which is why lacquer is gone. With lacquer, there was so much solvent used. In a large part of the country lacquer isn't available.

Is waterborne just around the corner, and how is that to work with?

Here Paul Stoll explains some fine point of paint and paint chemistry to Dave Perewitz.

Q&A Paul Stoll, PPG Trainer

By the end of 2008 it will be mandated in parts of California, and Canada is going the same way I think by 2010. There are advantages to waterborne. It will dry in two minutes and I can tape on it right away. Remember, this is waterborne not water-based. Water-based is latex. Waterborne is automotive, it's still acrylic urethane, it still has solvent, but uses water as the reducer. Actually it's de-ionized, mineral-free water, not water out of your tap.

Can you talk about single stage paints and compare them to basecoat-clearcoat systems?

Single-stage urethanes are resin-rich to pro-vide the gloss, they will require more coats to get color and are restricted to solid colors like red or white. To use them for a custom job you have to let it completely dry, then color sand, and then start in with art work.

They are durable because of the high load of resin. The extra resin makes them more flexible and chip resistant. In a multiple-color paint job though the single-stage paint will slow you down. A more popular choice for custom work is basecoat-clearcoat paints. Basecoats are ure-thane, but stronger in pigment with less resin so they cover faster. This means far less milage than with a single-stage paint. You will get quicker, multi-layer paint with less dry time between coats.

Should I catalyze the basecoats?

With a non-catalyzed base you don't have to sand between coats, you have an open window of time as to when the next coat is applied. If you catalyze the basecoat, you get a more chip-resistant film. The downside to catalyzing is it's a 24 hour win-dow to apply the topcoat, other-wise you have to sand before top-coating. For bike painting I would catalyze the basecoat. With a bike job you can get done with-in the 24 hour window. And then you would catalyze the clear.

You said the reducer is very important, can you expand on that?

Well, the reducer has 3 jobs: 1. To thin the paint to make it sprayable. 2. The reducer also controls the flash. The idea is that the surface of the paint stays open for two to five minutes so all the solvents evaporate at once. This is where your choice of reducer will make or break you.

If you are doing what you love, then it's easy to enjoy the work.

Q&A Paul Stoll, PPG Trainer

If it flashes off too quickly the solvents are trapped. Sometimes, if it's too slow you can actually tape out faster. Slow solvent is easier if you are spraying metallic and pearl, it provides more time to flow out. When you unmask, it won't pull paint. People use the wrong reducer all the time and it's a huge problem.

3. Allow the paint to achieve final leveling and begin the drying/curing process.

The reducer is made up of a mix of solvents. The most aggressive ingredient in the can makes up 60% of the reducer. This part evaporates out quickly, much of it before the paint actually hits the car. This is why you never leave the top off the can.

Tail solvents make up 10%, of the total solvents. The tail solvent evaporates out last, thirty days or more after the paint job is finished. Which is why you don't wax for 30 days, because you can trap the solvent.

For candies and peals, what are the flakes made of and what's the real difference?

Pearls were traditionally made from leaded material, but those are long gone, they were combination of shells. The new ones are made from mica. The manufacturer achieves different colors through the use of different coatings. The new latest, Crystal Pearls are made from aluminum oxide. They are far brighter and more chromatic than the earlier pearls.

People should remember that pearls have to be added in a transparent coat. You mix them in clear or a transparent color, like a mid-coat clear (DBC500), or in paint formulas that contain transparent toners only. Pearls can't be added to white or any opaque color that hides. Black is not opaque and pearl can be added to black.

In custom painting, pearls are often used over a white base to provide a brilliant base for candies, the brightest most chromatic color. Over a silver base it picks up a yellow color. Pearls are good to create great ghost effects and ghost flames.

If you put a pearl on top of a candy finish you loose the depth of the candy paint. Pearls can be added to metallic color to create a subtle effect, it will create additional brilliance and slight color shift. Color Pearls also shift opposite of the color wheel, blue shifts yellow, red pearl shifts green.

Can you talk about candy paint jobs?

Candy paint jobs can be done in basecoats or in topcoat urethane clear. Candies are traditionally made by adding a dye to the clear. Candy paint jobs can be achieved by mixing transparent toners and basecoat clear. Exceptions to using toners are candy apple red, candy orange or candy yellow. These colors are hard to make from paint toners. Transparent red, for example, is made from red oxide or blue-shade reds that create magenta shaded candies. Candy needs to be sprayed over a base that contains pearl or metallic for the full effect. Beginners should spray candy blue over blue metallic base, because it is easier to control. You get color quicker with less streaking and blotchiness. As painters get better they can go to gold or silver metallic base for the candy job.

Let's talk about application. When people work at home or in small shops, where do they fail? What are the critical conditions needed for good paint application, and what are some common mistakes?

Heat and air movement are the two big items. Catalyzed paint needs to be at a constant 60 degrees, or above, for 24 hours. You can't shut off the heat at night and then turn the heat back on in the morning. If the booth doesn't move enough air the solvent doesn't leave the paint, and you get solvent pop, or color dieback. They forget to keep notes as to what they sprayed, the base, the pearl, and all the rest, so they can repair the car or bike if they have to. And sometimes they mix brands. It's better to buy all the paint from one manufacturer, so you don't have trouble with incompatible products.

Chapter Six

One-Off Custom

A Basecoat/Clearcoat Job

We built this bike for a good customer, Brian Gould. Brian has owned a number of Perewitz bikes, and for this one he didn't want to stop half way. Brian wanted something more extreme than anything we'd built for him in the past, so we started with a long Low Life frame from Legends. Brian wanted some of the bike enclosed by panels, but he didn't want what you would normally call a "body bike." Big Ron, our metal man, fabricated the rear fender and body

I like our bikes to flow, and Brian's bike really does. Note how the tank blends into the rear fender body-section. The graphics reinforce the flow and help to carry the energy from the tank through to the rear fender.

section from sheet steel. For the gas tank Ron started with a tank from Legends which he stretched so it would flow right into the rear body section.

Where we come in to the photo sequence, Ron has the rear body-section finished and Jim has already applied three coats of filler. With each application of filler Jim works with a finer grade of sand paper. He started with 36 grit coarse paper on the first coat of mud, and ends with 80 grit, working with the sand paper wrapped around a flexible sanding pad.

Part of what you see in the nearby photos is Ron hand fitting the seat area to the custom seat we had made. Obviously he needs to make sure the seat opening is the right size before going too far with the body work on this part of the bike.

SPOT PUTTY

After three coats of filler and some careful sanding, we mix up some spot putty and use that to fill small low areas. This is easier than mixing another big batch of filler. We don't need to skim coat the whole thing again at this time.

Sanding the spot putty is done initially with a DA and an 80 grit pad, and then continues by hand with more 80 grit paper on a soft sand-

Seat area is very critical. Here you see Big Ron fine tune...

...the opening until the fit is absolutely perfect.

75

Finished seat is placed in pocket one last time.

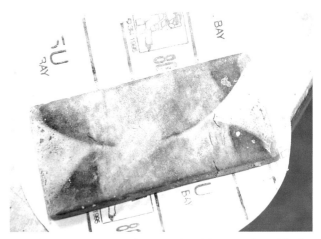

Sandpaper is wrapped around rubber sanding block to assure that they don't put finger marks in the filler while sanding.

Rear fender has shiny coat of plastic filler used to keep everything straight.

A round dowel is used with sandpaper for concave areas.

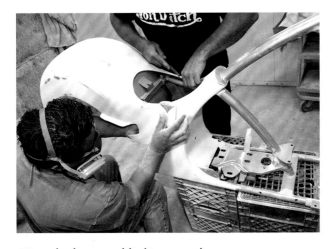

Here the boys are blocking out the putty.

It's important to remove plastic filler from all the edges.

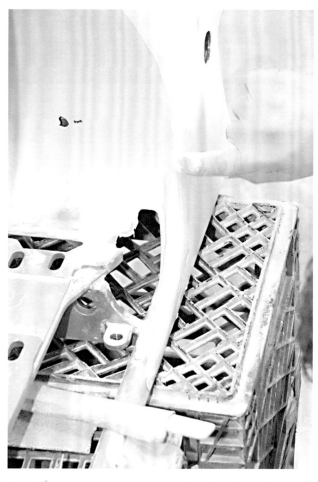

Radiuses are very important. Hand work is often required to get the necessary shape.

Here we are mixing the two-part spot putty.

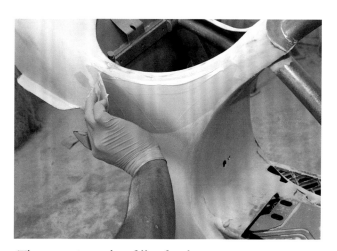

The putty is used to fill a few low spots.

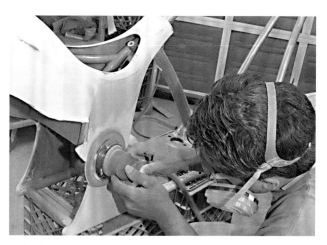

The first rough work is done with a DA equipped with 80 grit paper.

ing pad. The spot putty sands more easily than the heavier filler, and is generally sanded with the same grit of paper that was used just before on the filler.

For concave areas like under the seat we like to use a round sanding pad wrapped in the correct grade of paper, this way we're sure to get all the panels flat. Though there are plenty of power tools in the shop, sometimes you just have to do the work by hand. We also use the same round block to clean the filler from the edges of the sheet metal in the area under the seat.

Along the bottom of the frame, where the sheet metal meets the frame tubes, we apply some of the spot putty by hand, this is the only way to get a really nice radius in that area.

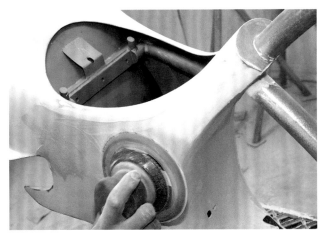

Always follow the shape, here we keep the sanding pad flat on a flat spot.

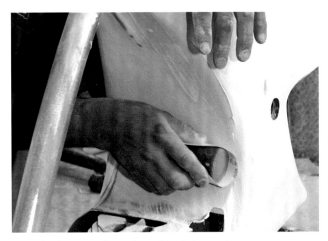

Here's the round sanding block in action.

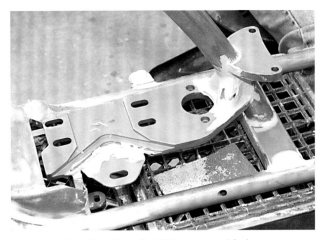

Details. Details. Details. We even mold the motor mount area.

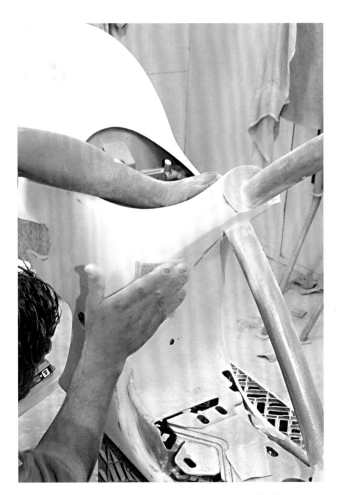

After sanding with the DA, we fine tune by hand using 80 grit.

PRIMER

Once we are happy with the filler, the spot putty, and the basic finish on the metal, it's time for four coats of two-part, high-solids primer. After we've given the primer enough time to fully cure, we apply a guide coat. This is just a light coat of black paint and it's called a guide coat because it acts as a guide for the block sanding. If there's any black paint still showing after the block sanding, that's a low spot that needs to be filled. After spraying on the black paint we start the sanding with 80 grit paper on a DA.

Even after going over the whole bike though, we still have to block sand everything with 220 grit paper. This block sanding is done with 220 grit paper and lots of water.

continued, page 82

Be careful when molding the neck that no plastic gets into the numbers, which must be readable when we're all done.

Here we've started wet sanding the primer.

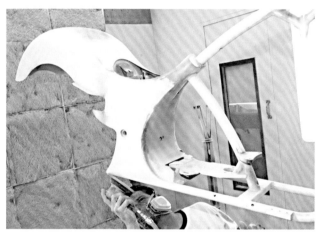

At this point we've sprayed four coats of two-part epoxy primer on the frame and rear body section, followed by a guide coat

During the block sanding, take your time, and keep the paper wet and clean.

Because of the guide coat, low spots and areas we haven't sanded yet show up dark.

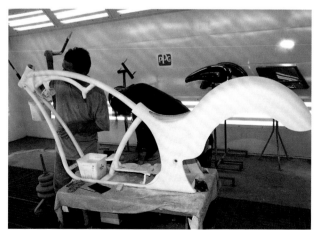

After spraying on an additional three coats of two-part primer, the guys do the final block sanding with 360 grit paper and lots of water.

Molding a Swingarm

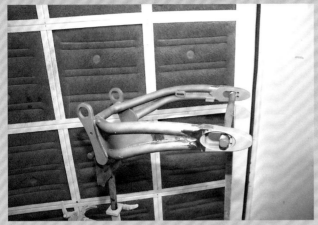

A good swing arm stand is a must. Note how we've sanded the areas where the filler will be applied so it sticks well to the rough metal.

Jay begins to take the excess filler off with 36 grit before the filler is completely dry, then finishes with 80 grit, working by hand.

Most of the small areas require that the plastic filler be applied by hand.

In some areas you can use a small DA equipped with 80 grit paper.

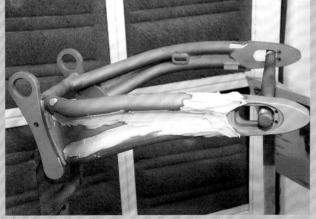

This is what the swingarm looks like after the first coat of filler.

Fine tuning needs to be done by hand.

Molding a Swingarm

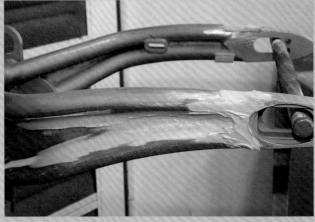

Time for a second coat of lighter filler, applied by hand.

After finishing off the second coat of filler with 80 grit, the swingarm is ready for primer.

Air tools can cut down on time, but we try to finish by hand.

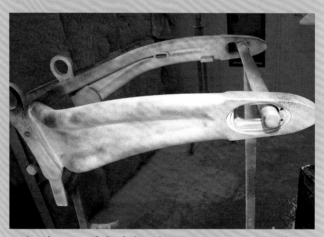

Like the rest of the bike, the swingarm is sprayed with three coats of primer-surfacer, then a guide coat to help us find any low spots.

As always, the finish work must be done by hand.

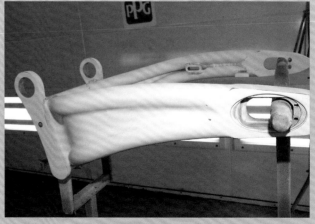

Nearly finished, the first coat of primer is sanded with 220 grit, now we're ready for second coat. Any good paint job is all about the details.

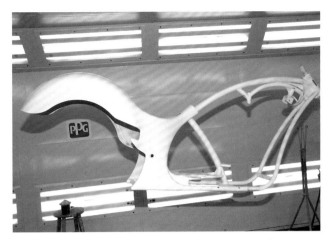

Finally we have the bike in the booth ready for paint. Almost.

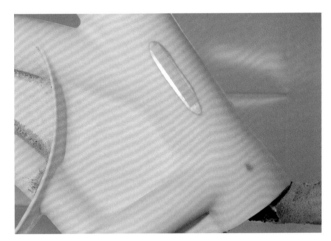

Be sure to keep the numbers visible, don't fill them with paint.

Jay puts on a coat of sealer, we use PPG Deltron DAS 3027 Dark Gray.

Jay wipes it down with cleaner. PPG-Spirit Wipe.

Once we have the frame down off the high bracket, the guys can work on the rear fender. They are still wet sanding with 220 grit, and because we put on a guide coat, any low spots will show up as dark areas.

MORE BLOCK SANDING

During the first round of block sanding we don't find any low spots, but we're not done block sanding yet. The guys apply another three coats of the two-part primer and let that cure overnight. Now they apply another guide coat of black and then start block sanding again. This time though, the flexible sanding pads are wrapped in 360 grit sand paper, used with plenty of water. The water flushes away the debris from sanding and helps the paper last a lot longer. When we do find a few small low spots, or pin holes, they are filled with spot putty.

As we've explained before in this book, you

Jay lays down a nice coat of dark grey sealer.

Now the tank is ready for paint.

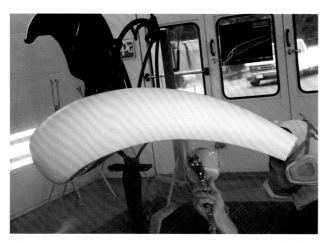

It's important to seal the bottom of the tank and the tunnel.

Here I'm putting on the first coat of PPG Blue Heaven

Always apply nice even coats, even with sealer and primer.

Frames are tricky to paint, take your time and be careful.

A good frame stand helps a lot and makes it easier to get at all parts of the tubing.

A good spray booth, well lit, helps too.

need a coat (or two) of sealer to separate the primer from the finish paint. Without sealer the bike might not all be the same color when the final paint is applied. Which means the final paint might not end up as a uniform color. And without sealer the finish paint that's applied may soak down in to the primer, which affects not only the color but the gloss of the topcoat.

MOTORCYCLE BLUES

We wait fifteen minutes for the sealer to dry before I start to apply the color. Be careful with sealer. Don't wait too long before applying the topcoat. Always be sure to work within the recommended topcoat window for that product. The topcoat I apply here is Blue Heaven urethane from PPG. It only takes two coats of the Blue Heaven to get the coverage I want. Because it's a urethane basecoat I can come back and apply the second coat pretty quickly after the first coat. We keep the shop at 70 degrees and the first coat is actually dry to the touch after only ten minutes.

Painting this frame and rear body section takes more time that you would think. It's hard to paint tubing, you have to come at it from a number of different angles to get good coverage. And then you have to be sure that you get the

Be sure to get good paint coverage everywhere, even under the fender.

Follow the shape of the object you are painting and keep the gun a consistent distance from the surface.

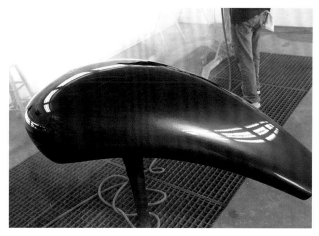

Here's the tank after three coats of clear...

I use long, even passes that overlap by 50%.

...the next job will be wet sanding with 500 grit, and then a trip to Keith Hanson's shop.

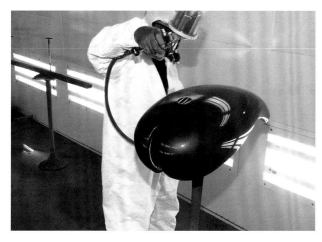

Each coat of base must flash before applying the next. If you go too fast you run the risk of trapping solvents.

I like clean and tasteful graphics.

Before he finishes, Keith pinstripes around the graphics.

Outlining the striping makes all the difference in the artwork.

areas under the rear fender and the bottom of the frame tube that are hard to see, and hard to paint.

CLEAR SAILING

As we explained early in the book, a basecoat/clearcoat paint job gets its gloss from the clearcoat. PPG offers a number of different clears, and for this job we use used their DCU 2042 clear. Paul Stoll likes to put it on a little wet, as he explains in his classes, "don't put the coats on light, put them on the way you want the paint to look."

After the clear dries we block sand it with 500 grit wet and then take it to Keith's shop for graphics. I like graphics that work with the lines of the bike, and these do. They also add a nice color accent. We almost always pinstripe the graphics, which makes them more interesting and complex.

The final task is to clear coat everything, including the artwork on the tank. Then we buff the clear for the best possible shine. This particular clear is nice because it doesn't get too hard too fast, which leaves us more time to do the buffing. It's a lot of work and, a lot of details to keep track of, but when it's all done we have a paint job you can'tget any other way.

Artwork is all outlined, but the tank still needs to be cleared for the last time.

This is a good look at the tank. I really like the way the tank meets the seat area, and how the graphics enhance the bike's nice lines.

Brian's bike was a big hit in Sturgis. Here we have it parked in front of the old Stone House Saloon at sunset.

Chapter Seven

Tank Tails & Custom Paint

The 2008 Bagger

When we planned to customize and paint this new Bagger, I thought it would be a relatively easy job. The sheet metal from Russ Wernimont is really high quality and has nice lines, and I thought we could just buy one of his extended tanks and maybe a pair of fenders, paint them and then add a few accessories and be done.

When the new 2008 Bagger came into the shop, we realized right away that the 2008 Baggers use a different frame and different sheet

Baggers are big bikes with a lot of real estate. So the job is more work, but when you get it right it makes for a big, bold and in this case, beautiful canvas.

Dino Petrocelli

88

metal than the 2007 and earlier bikes, and that the sheet metal I planned to use from Russ just wouldn't fit.

So I asked Big Ron to extend the tank, to put tails on it, and we would leave the fenders alone.

TANK TAILS

You can see how Ronnie used templates made from light board to design the extensions. These new tanks are funny, the shape is all in the bottom instead of the top, so we had trouble extending the tank and getting a shape that we really liked.

But eventually we did get a nice shape and Ron cut out the panels from sheet steel, shaped each one and then welded the extensions on the tank.

Ronnie and I both agree that on a deal like this you really have to have the seat, so you know exactly how the seat and the tank tails fit together.

Once the tails and the little inner panels are welded on with the TIG welder, Ron peels off the decals on the side of the tank, then Jay sands off the paint with a DA sander equipped with an 80 grit pad. We usually just send tanks like this out to be sand blasted, but we're in a hurry with this one so we took all the paint off with the DA sander. You have to be careful if you send sheet metal out to be sandblasted, If the guy running the blaster doesn't know what he's doing it cre-

This 2008 FL gas tank is being stretched in our shop. The factory made so many changes in 2008 models that no one makes a stretched tank.

Here you can see how Big Ron makes a cardboard template to cut the pieces for the stretched section of the tank.

After cutting and forming the sheet metal pieces they are TIG welded together.

The tank has to be contoured to meet the shape at the front of the seat.

We worked hard so the lines of the tanks flow smoothly.

The rest of the paint is removed with a DA (double action) sander. It really helps to have the tank mounted on a good stand when you do this.

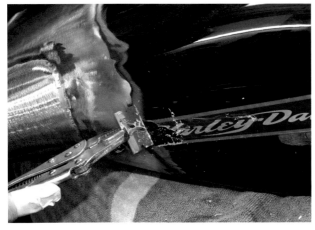

The Harley-Davidson decal is scraped off with a razor blade.

We did use our small sandblast cabinet to get the paint off of the bottom and the tunnel.

Here the bondo is carefully mixed up. If the two parts aren't thoroughly mixed you can get soft spots in the filler that never cure.

ates too much heat and the sheet metal can be warped as a result.

It's important that the weld seam be really clean, if there's any slag left in the seam from the welding that slag will eventually cause the filler to lift. Areas where there's a little bit of paint left, like the seams up around the filler neck, are OK. That paint is well bonded to the metal and our primer will stick to that paint no problem. The filler we use will stick to any metal, not all do, this stuff will stick to aluminum, or galvanized, or whatever."

MUDDY WATER

Jay puts on the first coat with the plastic spreader. He puts it on pretty neatly, so there isn't any more to sand off than necessary. And he starts sanding before it is fully set up. If you wait for it to get fully hard, you sand for days. How

Our choice is Evercoat for filler.

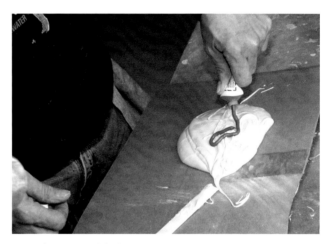

Hardener is added in exactly the amounts recommended by the manufacturer.

Mix until the batch has changed color and no blue hardening can be seen.

During the mixing, try to push down on the filler so any air bubbles are pushed out.

The first coat of Bondo is applied over the stretched area.

It's important to put on only as much as you need. Remember, any extra just has to be sanded off.

36 grit paper and a cheese grater are used to start off the sanding.

The plastic spreader makes it easy to follow the contour of the gas tank.

The first layer of filler gets roughed out with the 36 grit pad and a flexible pad.

4. *Here you can see how Jay sands the area where the filler meets the metal so there is no edge.*

1. *A second coat of filler is applied to smooth out the extensions.*

2. *Honestly, no fillers or additives.*

3. *36 grit paper again to get the basic shape.*

quick it sets up depends on the weather. You want it hard enough that you can't move it around. Jay uses a flexible sanding pad and 36 grit paper, but some people use a cheese grater to do the initial shaping.

The shaping goes pretty fast, because Jay has the tank on a sturdy fixture so he can really lean on the paper and the mud is sanded off quickly. When Jay is working this mud he has to know how much of the back of the tank will show and how much won't, so he knows which parts of the tank have to be finished really nice.

Once Jay has the first coat of filler smoothed out, he applies a second application. If you check the photos, you'll note that Jay is careful to put it on thinner this time. When he sands this second layer of filler, Jay uses long strokes to smooth and shape the mud, to get a nice flowing line.

When you're doing work like this, It's important to know how all the components fit, like the dash and the seat, so you know which areas have

It takes a keen eye to get a smooth finish.

Contour! Contour! Jay uses long, smooth strokes as the sanding pad follows the shape of the tank.

We like to finish the underside as well as the top. Detail work like this requires a little finger work.

Contour!

to be finished to a perfect smoothness.

If you look at the pictures, you notice that Jay goes so far as to mold the bottom of the tails, even though it's very unlikely anyone will ever see these areas.

After the second coat is sanded, Jay puts on one coat of Finishing putty. This material is lighter than the regular plastic filler and fills any little imperfections in the filler itself.

A COAT TO GUIDE US

When we get closer to the finish sanding I like to do a guide coat. As seen in the earlier chapter, this light coat of dark paint only takes a couple of seconds to apply and it shows you all your low spots where the dark paint doesn't get sanded off.

Jay sands the spot putty and the filler with 80 grit paper, on a flexible pad again. During the sanding, Jay spots a couple of very small low spots, which he fills with a second application of the putty. The second application is sanded with 80 grit, then Jay rolls the tank over and does a lit-

Finishing putty fills pinholes so you don't need as much primer.

The finishing putty is a nice way to smooth out the Bondo and fill any pinholes.

You shouldn't need much putty. Again, only use as much hardener as they recommend.

At this point the tank is sanded smooth and is ready for primer.

Apply a thin coat, you don't need to put the putty on very thick.

The K 38 is a great two-part primer.

Hardener is added per PPG's recommendations. The measuring cups make it easy to get the right amount of each component.

Here's the first coat of primer going on with an HVLP primer gun from DeVilbiss.

Three coats of primer should fill in the scratches.

After a guide coat is applied and the paint dries, the tank is wet sanded with 220 paper.

tle more finish work on the bottom.

Next, he blows it off with an air gun to get the dust off the surface, and out of any nooks and crannies.

THE FIRST COAT OF PRIMER

The primer we're using is K 38, a two-part primer from PPG. I like this primer because it's easy to sand and it will stick to anything. This is a high-solids primer that will help us get the panels really flat. Today we will shoot three coats of the primer, with a ten minute wait between coats, and block sand with 220 grit after the last coat has dried for three hours. Then we will shoot another three coats, let those cure overnight and then block sand again with 360 grit. Unless we see any little low spots or pinholes, the tank will be ready for paint at that point.

Slippery when wet! Jay is sanding the second application of primer with 360 grit paper.

Black basecoat to start.

Ready for sealer and then base coat.

Jay lays on the liquid metal.

Spraying sealer, DAS 3025 from PPG. This sealer comes in different colors, ideally you should pick a color close to the color of the basecoat.

Holy mother of Pearl! This will make a great base under the candy.

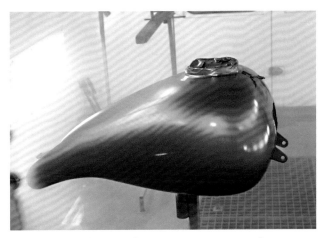

The watermelon candy goes on in a series of coats, and starts out pink.

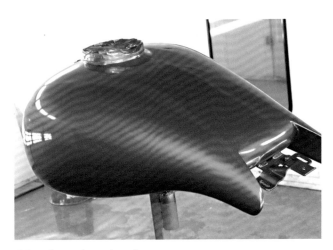

Note how the color changes...

...and gets darker with each successive coat.

SEALER

You have to put on sealer before the finish paint. This is mostly to make sure the topcoat doesn't bleed down into the primer or filler underneath. It also makes the tank one uniform color. The sealer comes in various shades of gray, the idea is to pick a color that's close to the top-coat color. We could have used a darker color here, but they were out of the dark grey.

Most sealers go on in one or two medium coats, and there is a window of time you have to pay attention to, a time period that's ideal for the application of the next coat of paint. In our case, the silver basecoat should go on within 15 minutes. If you apply basecoat a little too late, when the sealer is cross-linking, the basecoat can wrinkle. To check whether or not you've waited too long, drop a little "solvent" on the sealer and see if it wrinkles. If it does, wait another 90 minutes until the basecoat is applied.

BASECOAT AND CANDY

The basecoat we are using is DMD 1683 black. Jay puts on 3 good coats of basecoat, then waits about ten minutes before he can apply the next coat. Liquid metal is the next paint that we apply, this is a new silver basecoat that works really well under candys. The metallics in this liquid metal are ground very fine which gives it a much finer look than the old silver basecoat.

The liquid metal needs multiple light coats for good coverage. After waiting fifteen minutes we can apply the color. Because it's a candy it will take 6 to 8 coats to get good color.

The first two candy applications are really just a long series of light passes with the spray gun. After the first two coats are applied, the candy paint can be applied a little heavier.

Gradually the tank changes color from a light pink to a deep candy red. After a total of six coats Paul and I compare the color on the tank and the other parts with the PPG test panel, and decide that we have a match. The clear we use is 2042 from PPG and I put on a total of three coats. We let that dry overnight and then sand it the next

Is this the right tank? Oh, ya!

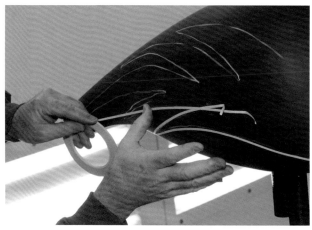

Paul works the thin masking tape across the tank, using the design I sketched out earlier as a guide.

The design should follow the shape of the tank.

Here we're trying to find the additional colors to be used in the graphics.

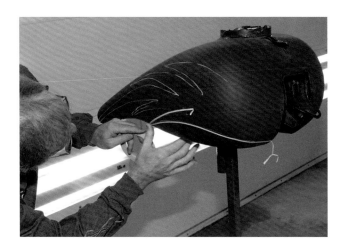

Paul and I both like to design the graphics right on the tank.

I think we got it, a good shape with a lot of motion.

3/4 inch tape is used for the outline, then use 1/8 inch tape to smooth out the curve.

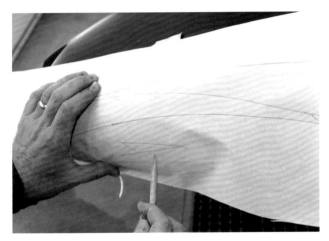

Here we're tracing the design to use on the other side of the tank.

The Pounce wheel makes tiny holes in the paper so the chalk can pass through.

morning with 500 grit paper wet. And now we're ready for the best part of the paint job.

THE FUN BEGINS

I like to design the graphics right on the tank or panel. One of the hard parts is finding colors that work with the basecolor, the watermelon in this case. Paul and I use color chips of PPG colors to find a shade we like. We hold them up against the tank, one at at time, until we find the perfect color.

I like 1/8 inch tape, or sometimes wider tape if it's a long line, because it's not as likely to kink. And I like to use masking tape during layout like this because you use a lot of it. The wider masking tape tends to make a nicer radius, it's nice when you are starting out. Sometimes I use the wide tape to check the radius of the thin tape.

Once we have a basic design that we like, Paul makes a template of the design from a sheet of light paper. A template like this is a good way to duplicate the pattern on the other side of the tank, and to transfer the design to the bags.

The way we do it is pretty low-tech. The little pounce wheel punches a long series of small holes in the template, (check the nearby photos) then the chad is knocked off the backside with a piece of sand paper or a razor blade. Next we hold the template up against the side of the tank or the bag and tap a little homemade "pounce pad" against the template. The pounce pad (which can be purchased in an art-supply store) contains colored powder that transfers through the holes in the template to leave a tracing of the design on the tank or the bags. This tracing makes it easy to tape out the design on the other tank side and on the bags.

Once the design is transferred you have to cutout the "overs and unders", the places where the 1/8 inch tape goes too far. This is always harder than it seems. As Paul explains, "sometimes with a complicated design I just stop for a minute to figure out where everything is going." Once the outline of the design is complete we do all the rest of the taping with wider masking tape. With larger areas you can use masking paper for this.

Tools of the trade, the pounce wheel, available at any art store in different sizes with different diameter pins.

With the template in place, we "pounce" the paper. The little porous bag of chalk, or pounce pad, is rubbed against the holes in the template...

By running sand paper across the back side of the template the little tabs of paper, or "chad" are knocked off leaving a clean pin-hole.

The track of chalk dust is left behind after the paper template is removed.

Here we position the template on the saddle bag.

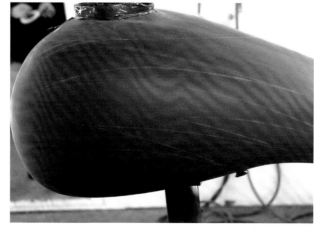

You can see how we've done the same thing on the left side of the tank. This way the art is consistent throughout the bike.

Once the layout is done we can start masking off the rest of the tank.

The tank is ready for the second color.

Tank is being wiped down before spraying. Put some cleaner on the rag, wipe and then come back with a dry rag. Always wipe back to front so you don't roll back any of the tape-tips.

Special sauce! Body wash. This water-borne cleaner works better than solvents as it will clean off the oils from your hands and any finger prints.

GRAPHICS

After looking at all the color cards, we decided on a gold color, DBC 25622, as the base for the graphics. Paul wipes the tank down with a water borne cleaner and it's time to shoot.

The gold is put on in four coats,, with about a ten minute wait times between each coat. Now we get out the big metal flake and mix it with DBC 500, intercoat clear. The flake should be mixed so it's 5% flake by volume. We add two tablespoons of the flake to ten ounces of the DBC 500. After the first application of flake, we wait for 20 minutes and look the job over. There seems to be too much space between the flakes so we add a second coat. The previous coat should be dry to the touch before adding another coat of the flake, and intercoat clear.

We end up putting on three coats of the flake

Gold base is applied with an HVLP gun.

Here were' applying speed-lines in orange with the airbrush.

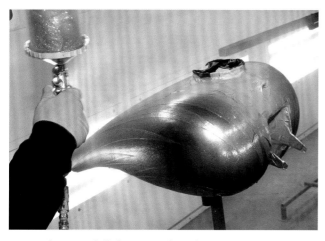

Next the metal flake, mixed with intercoat clear, is applied over the gold base. It rook three coats of the flake to get the coverage we wanted.

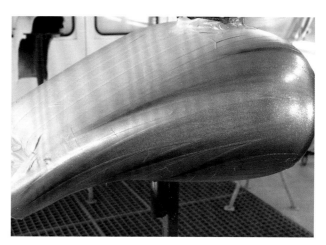

The idea is to create speed lines inside the scallops that are darker at the tips.

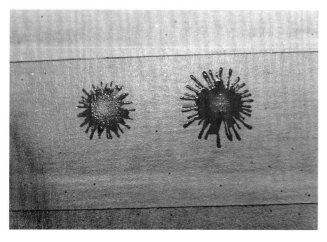

Before using the airbrush, we need to check the pattern. These are good.

Here we are putting on a light application of yellow.

The yellow gives the gold some real punch, the whole thing is much brighter.

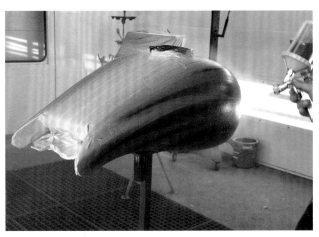

Except that I want to add just one more blast of yellow as the final coat of paint.

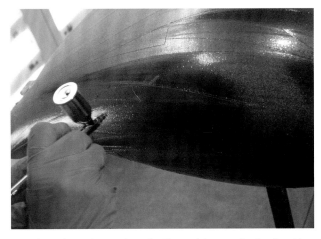

With red in the airbrush, I'm adding a little detail and making the tips darker.

Removing tape is always fun. Fun to see what you've really created.

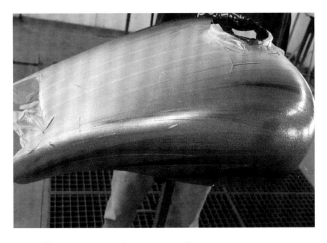

Finally we are ready to unmask.

Great colors! I love the contrast.

Even the bottom of the tank and bags need to be cleared.

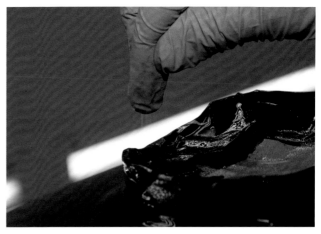

The touch test! You want it just dry enough to string up when you touch it.

Here the artwork is cleaned and the clear coat is applied (Vibrance VC5200).

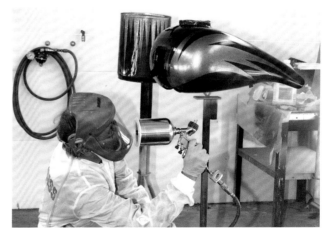

The entire tank is cleared.

mix. The gun is a DeVilbiss, HVLP unit equipped with a 2.2mm tip. As Paul likes to say, "The flake should not be put on dry, and should not be put on with a small tip, you want to get it out so it lays flat and reflects lots of light. You don't want to dust it on, and you don't want it to have random orientation and stand at all types of angles because you get dark spots that way."

MORE DETAILS

There's really no limit to what you can do when you do a custom paint job. We could have just stopped after the metal flake, but I thought it would be good to add some more motion to the scallops. So Paul and I added speed lines to the scallops with a DeVilbiss airbrush and some orange.

Remember, you are only limited by your imagination. Next we apply some yellow, over the whole graphics area, with a small mini-jet spray gun. This application of the yellow makes the flakes, the whole thing, much brighter and creates a more intense yellow/gold color.

When cleaning metal flake - more coats of clear are usually necessary to bury the flake.

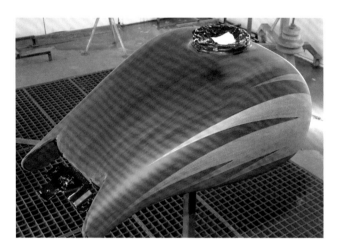

At this point the tank is cleared and sanded with 500 grit paper. It's ready for pinstripe artwork.

Cleared ready for sanding and the application of finish clear.

The final touch is applied with the airbrush again. This time it's red from the PPG Spectraflame line, and we use it to add detail to each speed line and darken the tips. And finally we give the whole thing one more coat of the yellow.

PULL THE TAPE

When we pull the tape there are some ragged edges. If we had let the paint dry we wouldn't have those, but I can blow the hanging pieces off with air. And of course the pinstripes will be used to clean up the edges. If you try to take the little loose pieces off with your hands you end up pushing it against the tank, and then they stick to the tank.

People are sometimes amazed at how many steps are involved in custom painting. After we pull the tape and blow off any hanging pieces of paint, we have to clear the tank again. Four coats of clear will bury the art work nicely so there are no edges. After it's sanded with 500 grit it will provide a nice surface for Keith Hanson to put down those great pinstripes (see the next chapter).

After the pinstripes, the job comes back to the shop for six more coats of clear applied in two, three coat applications. We sand with 600 grit after the first three coats, then apply another three. The final buffing process starts with 2000 grit wet after the last coats of clear are cured. If you have orange peel, though, you need to start with 600 – 800 wet paper, and work up to 2000. When we are finished sanding with 2000 we start the buffing, which is covered at the end of Chapter Nine.

Three good coats of clear, after striping, will bury artwork. Then we do the final clear with three more coats.

The contrasting colors, the flake, and the pinstripes all come together when you finally roll that paint job out into the sun.

Dino Petrocelli

Chapter Eight

Pinstripes with a Flair

The Work of Keith Hanson

Keith Hanson has done nearly all the pinstriping and much of the graphics on my bikes for a number of years now. Keith's work is very nice, and a little outside of the box. This set of pinstripes is a good example. Instead of just laying down a set of stripes that outline a graphic or set of flames, Keith lays down a very thin and precise set of pinstripes made up of variegated gold leaf. Then he outlines that with a second, more traditional, pinstripe.

Using gold leaf as a pinstripe material means first laying down what looks like a gold pinstripe

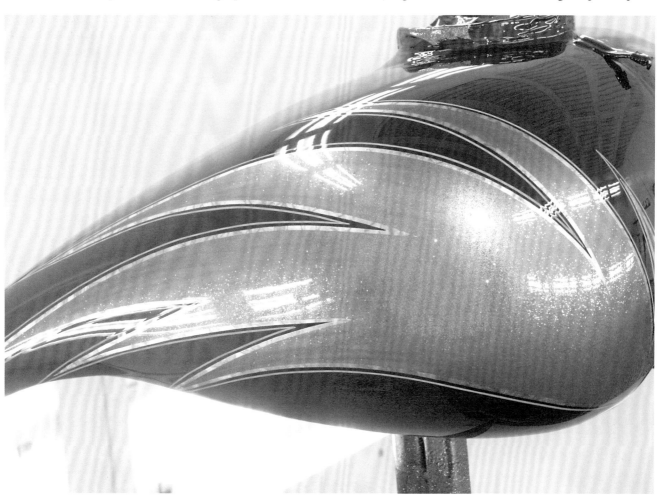

The finished tank seen in the paint booth immediately after the final application of clearcoat. A nice custom paint job requires a long series of steps, each one must be done correctly and in the right sequence or the end result will disappoint.

with a standard Xcaliber brush. In reality, the pinstripe paint is a mix of One-Shot paint and Rolco size. Size is the adhesive commonly used when applying gold leaf to larger surfaces.

Once the gold "pinstripe" is sufficiently tacky, Keith pushes the sheet of gold leaf up against the sticky adhesive and then begins to gently pull off the excess leaf. He continues this process until the entire graphic is surrounded by a very thin stripe of gold leaf.

Once he's done with the gold leaf, Keith lays down one more, very thin pinstripe. When it comes to colors, Keith chooses colors that often seem to be a little off the mark. But once he lays down that first stripe you realize that his color choice is always right on.

People might think that the gold leaf would make for a really big bump on the tank, and that it would be hard to bury that in clear, but it's really not any worse that a standard pinstripe job. The outside pinstripe on this job is done with House of Kolor urethane striping paint, which dries pretty fast. After the H of K paint is dry we can wipe the tank down and start the clearcoating. There's no need to wait for the paint/size used under the pinstripes to dry or cure for a long time.

Once Keith is finished, we take the tank back to the shop and apply four coats of clear, which is then sanded, and buffed.

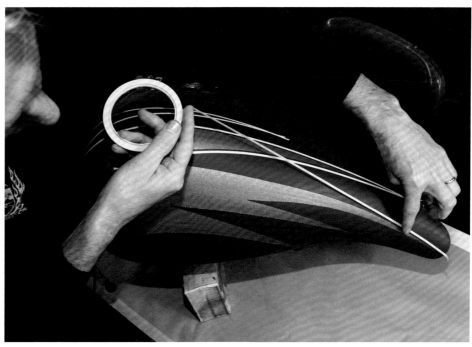

1/8 inch masking tape is laid down approximately 1/8 inch from the graphic that is to be striped. It will be used as a guide.

Captions by Keith Hanson

Holding the roll of tape in one hand, use the other hand to guide and secure the tape to the panel.

Let the tape overlap at intersections...

...this is so you can see your striping when the size is clear. After smoothing the paint on the brush with your fingers, use a pallet to work paint up into the brush.

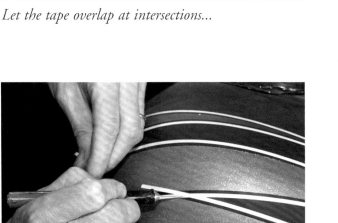

...then trim them with a sharp x-acto blade. Just score the tape and it will come right off.

Once the brush is ready, use the tape as a guide. Do not touch the tape with the brush.

The first stripe will be variegated gold leaf, so the striping will be done with Rolco quick size mixed with 1-Shot imitation gold paint...

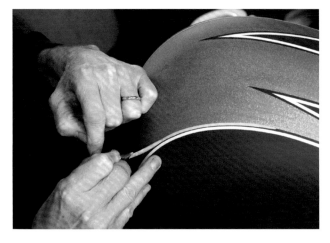

Hold your fingers lightly on the surface to steady your hand - using the other hand if necessary...

...this is helpful especially when coming to the end of intersecting lines.

Keep track of your time so that you don't lose the tackiness of your size.

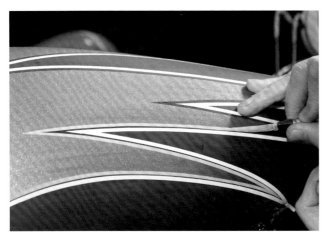

Make sure that intersecting lines are sharp and clean.

Again, use your other hand to support your striping hand.

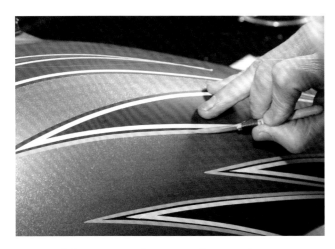

Be careful not to touch previously striped areas - smudges are difficult to clean up.

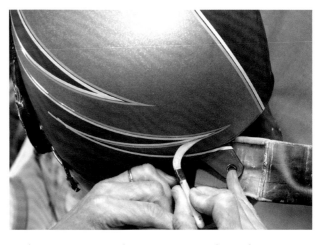

Take your time at the intersections, keep the tips clean and sharp.

Q&A: Keith Hanson

Keith Hanson is the man responsible for the beautiful and unusual goldleaf pinstripes seen on many Dave Perewitz paint jobs, as well as the graphics that can only be called wild and innovative. When everyone else is working to ensure the design on one side of the tank is the exactly the same as what's on the other side, Keith is intentionally tweaking his designs to ensure that one side is *not* the same as the other. The man who started out with a route as a milk man has a lot to say about not only pinstriping, but the design behind pinstriping as well. Part of the material that follows is from an earlier Wolfgang book: *Advanced Pinstripe Art.*

Keith, How did you make the break from milk-man to full time pinstriping and airbrushing?

I was already pinstriping on my day off, and then one day I did a Falcon for the foreman at the dairy. He came out when I was done, took a long look, at what I'd done, and said. "what are you doing delivering milk for a living?"

When I did go out on my own I came across a company that did detail work at dealerships. Next I stared working with John Hartnett. We did a lot of race cars. Eventually I made the transition from racecars to motorcycles. It was about the same time I met Dave Perewitz and now I do a lot of work for Dave.

Where do you get your ideas and inspiration?

I try to get ideas and influence from outside of the automotive and custom motorcycle industries. You have to stay fresh. People go to car of bike magazines for inspiration, but then they just recycle ideas. The art museum is good. The fashion industry comes in handy as there are so many top designers to choose from. The challenge is to find a way to start with a design that's on canvas and take it to metal, you need different products and processes.

Do you pre-plan the design?

I always start from a tight center and work my way out, there is no true pre-planning other than to decide how much space it's going to take up. If you go too far out to begin with you have a lot of space to fill. Better to start tight, you can always add a bit if you need to.

Knowing when to say when is important so you don't add something to a design that you wish later you hadn't. I like to look at it, step back and ask, 'is there anything I can do to improve on that?' in the case of a graphic design, the pinstripes can really pull things together.

Working in a small shop outside Boston, Keith Hanson does everything from pinstripes to elaborate airbrush designs.

Q&A: Keith Hanson

What do you like to use for a brush?

Xcaliber, size 00, I don't change the brush, other than to cut out a stray hair. I use one brush for everything. I find I can get a line that's 1/8th or 1/16th inches wide, or anything in between with that same brush. Why change brushes if I don't have to?

So the number of the brush doesn't correlate to the size of the line?

There is a correlation, but if you use the brush right you can get more than one size of line.

You use an extra piece of tape, is it a guide?

Yes, that thin piece of tape is a guide, you don't touch it, it's just a guide.

Are straight lines harder than curves?

Yes, long straight lines are hard, keeping them consistent is a challenge, some people have trouble with tight curves.

Is there a trick to doing really nice consistent lines.

Practice, patience and perseverance. There are no shortcuts.

Do you do any teaching?

I do a class for Bear Air. I find though that people don't always pay attention at the beginning, they don't realize how hard it is to lay down a nice line.

Do you ever wipe off a line and start over?

Yes, I just did in fact. But I very seldom do it. You don't make any money that way. Sometimes I do something unusual in a design sense and then see how I can get myself out of it. It forces me to be more creative.

How do you pick your colors for the pinstripes?

It depends, whether I'm looking for contrast or for blending. Typically I like to add to the visual impact so I go for contrast. I think of Miami and the architecture and how colors that you don't think would work well together do. I don't get off on doing things that are subtle, what's the point.

I like bright color, full designs. They won't walk across the street to look at the same old thing.

After many years of collaboration, there's an easy and respectful give and take between David and Keith.

Carefully use the x-acto to pick up tape edges and slowly lift the tape off the tank.

Apply the leaf gently, taping it into place with your fingertips.

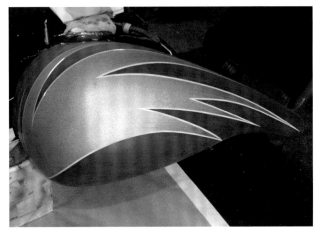

Once the tape is removed wait approximately 15 minutes (check tack with the back of your finger).

It's OK to pick up the excess pieces of gold and apply them to another section of striping.

When you feel some tackiness, but no paint comes off on your finger, you're ready to apply the gold leaf.

Don't use pieces that are too small - there will be too many rough edges if you do - expect some waste.

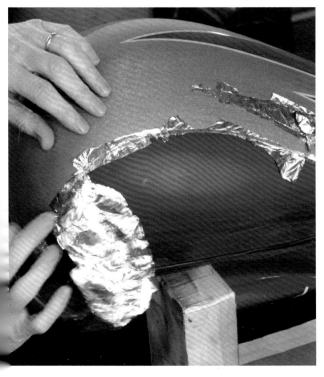

Wait till you have applied all the leaf before you begin to wipe the excess off.

When tapping down the leaf be careful not to smudge the size.

Keep track of the striping so it doesn't dry before you apply the leaf ...

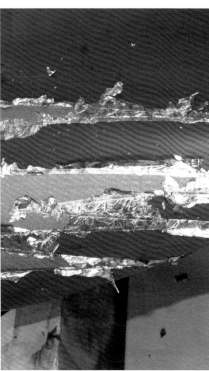

...now all the leaf has been applied...

...a well worn tack cloth works well to remove the excess leaf, don't apply too much pressure.

The second stripe will be done with H of K striping paint, the color is peach U-28.

The second line is about 3/32 inch away from the leaf and is thinner than the other, about 1/16 inch.

Carefully use the leaf as a guide...

Following the gold leaf is a little more difficult than using the tape as a guide...

...with practice and patience you can do it.

...concentration is key, especially when you get to the tips and intersections.

When some of the graphics are low, or under the surface, it helps to turn over the tank.

Some angles can be tricky, go slowly and concentrate.

Use a soft towel to lay the tank on so you don't scratch the surface.

It helps to support your hand with the other one.

Continue to pallet your brush to keep the paint flowing smoothly, you can feel the viscosity as you draw the brush across the pallet.

Keep the brush sharp at the tip to keep the lines clean.

Lightly rest your fingers on the surface for support.

Always make sure that the tips are clean and sharp.

Your patience will pay off when you see your completed job.

The finished striping helps detail and accent the graphics making for a clean and complete paint job.

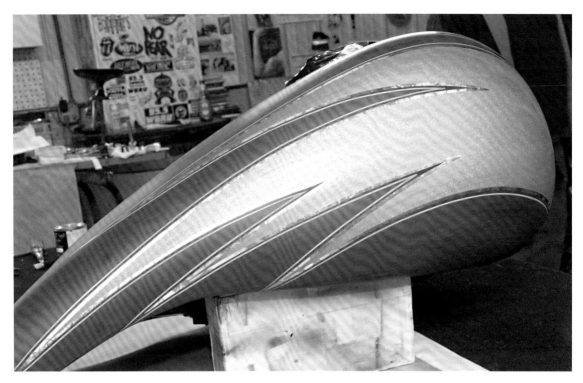

The finished tank, before the final clearcoats.

And after the clearcoats. A lot of work, but well worth the effort.

Chapter Nine

Dave's 2007 Bagger

A Heavenly Paint Job

The sheet metal you see us working on here is part of a 2007 Bagger project we built recently. The tank and fenders are from Russ Wernimont. Russ' parts are well made and don't require much in the way of body work or finishing – unlike some other brands. We did apply three coats of two-part primer, which Jay block sanded with 220 grit. Then we put on another three coats of primer and block sanded everything one more time with 360 paper.

This is the finished 2007 Bagger we built. And though the bike is lowered and rolls on aftermarket wheels, it's the paint, and the paint design, that makes this a great looking motorcycle.

Where the photos start we are applying one coat of sealer, which in this case is DP 90 from PPG. As always, we apply the first coat of the topcoat paint within the prescribed time window recommended by the manufacturer.

The basic color for this bike will be blue, and the specific paint is DBC basecoat blue heaven from PPG. We've added some blue-to-purple color shifting pearl to the paint for a special effect. Because we've added the pearl, it's important to strain this paint more thoroughly than you would a non-pearl paint.

This basecoat is catalyzed with DX 57 catalyst. We mix 1-1/2 ounce of the catalyst per ready-to-spray quart. The reducer in this case is 885, chosen because the temperature in the shop is about 80 degrees.

For a spray gun we've chosen a new Tekna HVLP gravity feed gun equipped with a 1.3mm fluid tip. Because the blue heaven is a basecoat, it dries pretty fast and within ten minutes we can apply the second coat. No matter which gun you use, it's a good idea to check with the gun manufacturer to see what the maximum recommended pressure is. It's a good idea to check the pressure at the gun with the trigger pulled, with one of the small gauges that mount at the base of the gun.

Jay wipes things down with a tack rag after block sanding for the last time and before applying the sealer.

We always start applying the sealer to the undersides first.

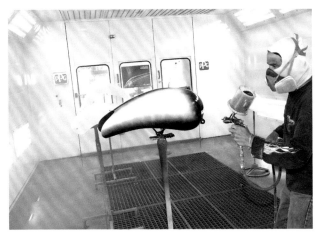

Here Jay starts on the rest of the gas tank.

Working within the designated time-window, the next step is application of the blue heaven basecoat.

Jay overlaps each pass by 50% as he applies the DP 90 sealer to the rest of the tank.

The basecoat dries pretty quickly and the second coat can go on about ten minutes after the first.

All the parts have to be coated with sealer. Typically it takes one, or possibly two, coats of sealer to get good coverage.

The first coat of basecoat dries without much gloss. (this paint is still wet), and we have pretty good coverage after the first coat.

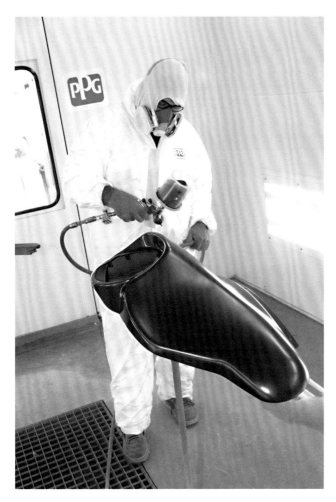

All the parts are painted at the same time so the coverage is uniform.

When the second coat dries we put on three medium coats of urethane clear. This is the new Vibrance clear number VC5200, it should be applied in three medium coats in stead of the old trick of applying one light and two heavier coats. If you try that with this newer clear you will get orange peel.

Once the clear is totally dry, we wet sand the tank with 500 grit paper on a soft pad. As we've mentioned before, without the soft pad it's easy to put grooves in the paint from the pressure of your fingers. Sanding with 500 grit will give us a nice surface, one that the next coat of paint can stick to.

Notice the way we keep the gun 90 degrees to the surface, even on curved sheet metal like this fender.

Here, I'm applying the second coat of blue heaven...

...to the tank.

Here I'm applying the final coat of blue heaven to the fender.

Color always looks better after the clear coats.

Here's the tank after the last coat of blue heaven and before we apply the clear.

Here I'm wet sanding block with 500 grit paper and a soft sanding block.

We put on three coats of the Vibrance clear, to ensure that we have enough clear to sand without sanding through.

The fairing is wet sanded with Ivory soap.

124

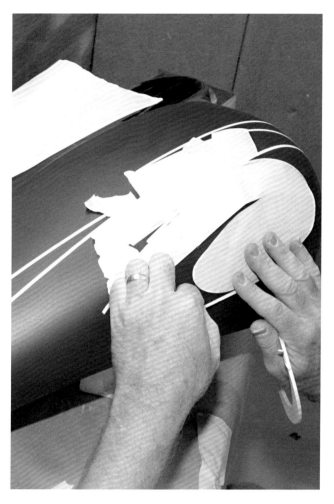

4. Once we have a design we like Paul makes a simple template which can be used to transfer the design and the dimensions to the other side of the tank.

DESIGN WITH TAPE

After wiping off the water and soap residue we can begin drawing out the graphics. As we've done on the other projects in this book, we start with tape, drawing out the design right on the tank. The hard part is getting the design to be the same from one side to the other. Sometimes Keith designs them to be a little different on purpose, but here we want them to be as close to identical as we can get them.

With the bags Paul draws out the design with masking tape on one bag, and then makes a template. This is quite similar to what we did with the 2008 Bagger and the template is used to layout exactly the same design on the other bag. As Paul explains, "I like making a template because

1. All pieces are wet sanded with 500 grit before artwork.

2. We design right on the tank with 1/8 inch tape.

3. To keep it all even we ran a piece of tape straight across the front, and then measure off the width of 2 fingers.

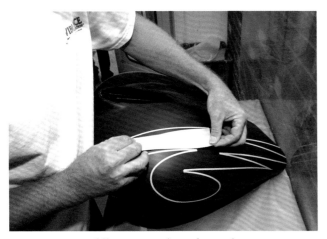

Now we start filling in with wide masking tape.

Here the design is laid out on one of the bags.

it goes faster than if I eyeball it. When I'm trying to be symmetrical I can just make a pattern and I'm done. And I'm used to working on cars, so in that case it's a lot of work to walk from one side to the other again and again to check that the design and the placement is the same."

GRAPHICS

The design or layout is done with thin 3M masking tape. The problem with plastic tape is it stretches too much. For spraying basecoats this tape sticks plenty good. The plastic tape is nice in the sense that it leave a cleaner edge. But even if we end up with fuzzy edges here, the edges will be covered up by the pinstripes so it doesn't matter. Once the design is laid out we mask off the top of the tank with wide masking tape and get ready for the next step in this paint job.

For the bottom of the tank, Paul mixes a rainbow flake from PPG, with DBC 500, intercoat clear. The rainbow flake makes up 5% of the mix which is reduced with DT 885 at 1:1 or 100%. Once mixed, the rainbow flake can be sprayed as a basecoat. It will takes us four coats to cover the heavenly blue, though if we were spraying over a uniform silver color it would only take two coats.

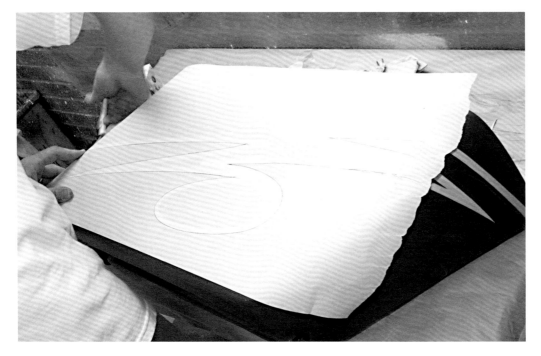

We take a pattern off the bag so we can transfer it to the other side.

126

Pattern is cut and laid out, and traced with chalk.

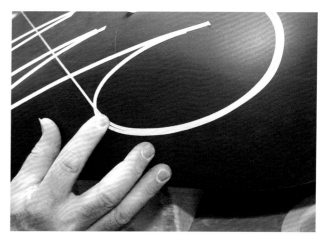

The 1/8 inch line is doubled with a second line for an in between color.

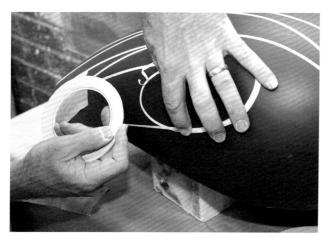

Here the outline is getting fattened up.

Outline is now 1/4 inch wide between colors.

Second stripe just follows the pattern.

Design is being filled in with a 2" tape, and cut with an X-acto blade.

Top half of the tank is masked now and ready for the next color.

Now we start spraying the rainbow flake mixed with DBC 500 intercoat clear.

PPG midcoat really glows - this is after only one coat.

BACK MASKING

At this point we have the top of the tank painted blue and the bottom painted with the spectra flair. Paul and I decided during the design phase to separate these two colors with a stripe of antifreeze green. For part of this strip we can just pull a thin piece of the tape laid down originally, (note the nearby photos) then on the front and back of the tank we have to mask out the rest of the stripe. If you follow through the photos all of this will make more sense. This part of the project points out the importance of thinking through the job before you start. By planning ahead during the layout and taping you can save a lot of work later.

Before we do anymore masking, we put another coat of intercoat clear on the spectra flair, to protect the paint during taping. Once that's dry we can tape the bottom of the tank and leave a stripe separating the two colors.

The antifreeze green is a candy color, part of the PPG Hot Wheels line, and we apply three coats with a small touch up gun. To give the stripe a little more visual impact, we load up a small amount of bright emerald, another Hot Wheels color, in an airbrush and carefully shade the lower edge and ends of the green stripe.

Now it's time to pull the tape and then clean and clear the tank. After the clear is dry, we sand all the parts with 500 grit wet, and then send them over to Keith Hanson's shop for pinstripes. After the pinstripes it's time for more clear.

FINAL CLEAR AND BUFFING

When the parts come back from Keith's we start by washing them down with soap and water. The next step is three coats of clear. When those three coats are dry, we wet sand all the parts with 600 grit paper on a flexible pad. Now we apply another three coats of clear, but for these last coats we over reduce the clear slightly. When those are dry we wet sand with 2000 grit paper. The buffing is next, and we start with a Meguiars compound and a foam pad. The final step is a finer foam pad used with a glazing compound. We wipe it down with a soft cloth and the parts are done.

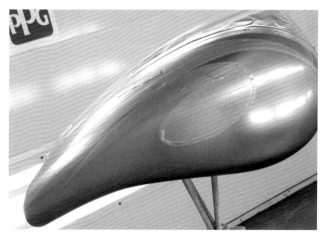

This is the tank with four coats of rainbow flake over the silver base. We put on one coat of DBC 500 intercoat clear before we start the masking.

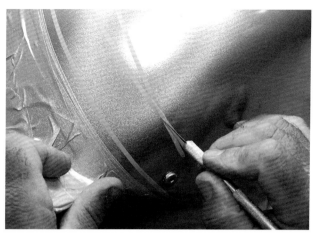

For points where the 1/8 inch tape crosses, cut the top piece first then cut along the second piece to form a pouch.

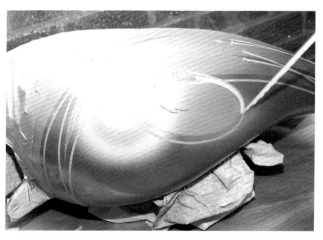

This is where planning ahead pays off. Here we pull the strip of tape laid down earlier, in order to leave a strip that will be painted antifreeze greene.

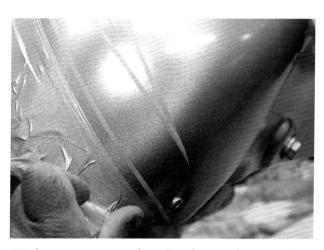

We leave approximately 1/4 inch space between the tape lines for color.

Creating the full stripe requires additional masking. I like using the X-acto to cut tape, but some guys and gals like a single edge blade.

Now the lines are back masked.

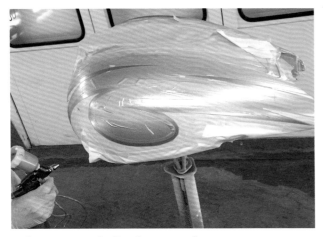

Job is now ready for the next color.

The darker green gives the stripe a subtle contrast.

Anti-freeze green is next, applied with a small touch up gun.

The fun part, removing tape!

The tips are then airbrushed with a darker candy green.

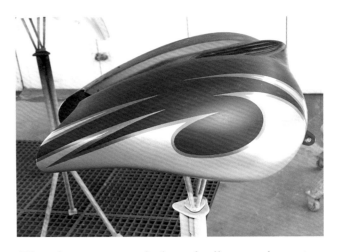

The job is starting to look good, all we need now is some pin striping to outline the colors.

130

The final clear is 2042 from PPG, applied in two, separate, three-coat sequences. The multiple coats of clear, and the sanding we do between the applications, makes for a perfectly smooth paint job. Combined with the buffing, the process leaves an incredible finish.

Never underestimate what you can do with paint. A good custom paint job is the simplest, and most effective, way to separate your bike from all the other bikes in the parking lot or at the bike show.

Chapter Ten

Flame Sequence

Proportion and Flow

When I do a layout for a set of flames, I make sure all the flames flow correctly. The little things are so important, all the curves and all the tips have to be in the right places. That's very, very important to the proportion of the flames. Sometimes you overlook one lick or one tip and don't notice it until it's all masked out. But even if I notice it after the taping is all done, I still back up and change that flame, I make it fatter or make it shorter or whatever is needed. That's really your last chance to make any corrections.

Good flames are all in the eye. There are no

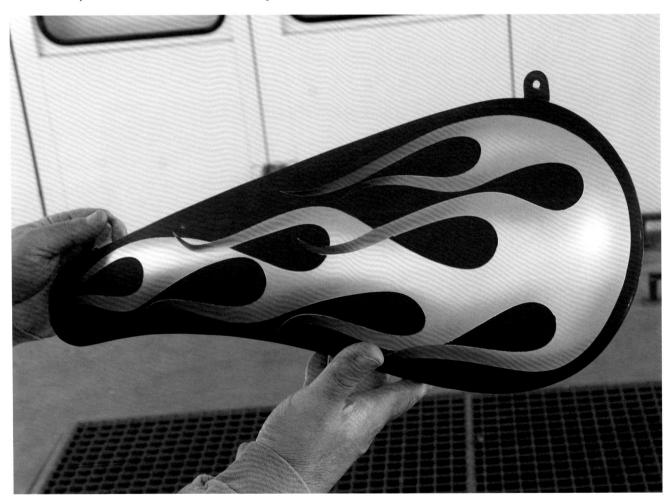

This panel is called a trophy tank. It's hand formed sheet metal in the shape of a gas tank, with tabs on top to hang it up. This one is painted, plus flamed, ready to be pinstriped. We do them mostly for charity auctions. They sell for as much as $4,000.

set rules. You have to trust your eye and you have to know how it's going to look when the job is all done.

Once you put the base on, then the work is done with the airbrush. For a typical flame job I might start with orange over a yellow base. The second color will be red, blended into the yellow. Then I finish with purple. Again, I'm careful to blend the purple into the red. Then I go back over the whole job with orange. I apply the orange carefully, just where it needs it. Anyplace the job needs a smoother transition.

I think the hardest part for people starting out is to get the flames to flow smoothly. That is the key. You have to do the layout so the tips are in the right place, that's the most important thing. Pay attention to where the tips end in relation to each other, and make sure there are no flat spots in the layout. There should be a radius on all the lines, all the lines are curves, there should be no straight lines.

The one thing people should remember when they start out doing flames, is to stand back for a really good look after the layout is done. Sometimes you can't see the straight line or the fault in the layout until it's all taped out and you stand a few feet back from the layout. Then don't be afraid to change the layout until you're really happy with the way it looks.

After the panel is painted with a base coat I start laying out flames with 1/8 inch masking tape. I usually start at the bottom and work up.

Some painters like the green tape, I prefer to use regular 1/8 inch masking tape. I like the way it bends and corners.

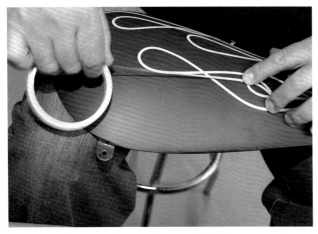

Pushing down with one finger while laying tape outs holds shapes in place.

Outline is looking uniform, crossovers always look good.

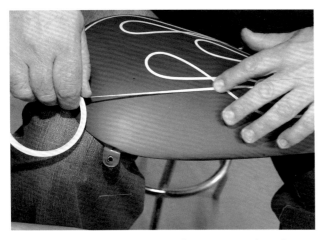

Make sure all lines in flames have a smooth radius, not straight lines.

Make sure flames gradually get wider.

Bending tape lines around just takes practice.

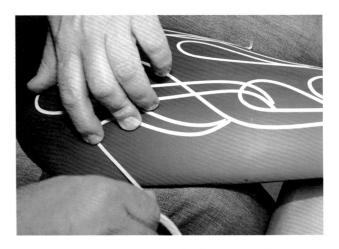

As you get close to top start thinking about how to end the flames.

Now we are at the top, make sure you don't run out of room.

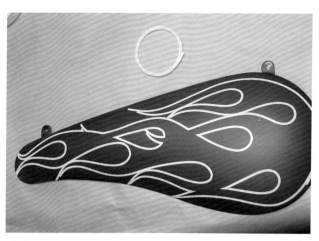

After cutting the crossovers out we are ready to mask the outside of the flames.

You don't want to run the flames off the top, and allow for striping.

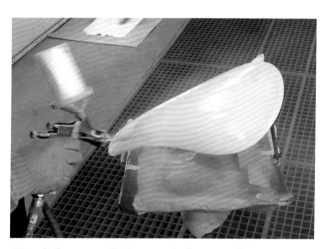

Two light coats of white with the DeVilbiss SRI gun is the first step.

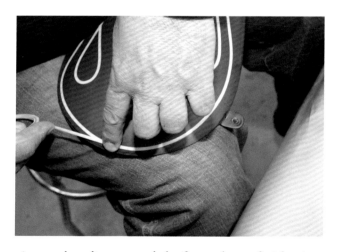

A smooth radius around the front always finishes it off nice.

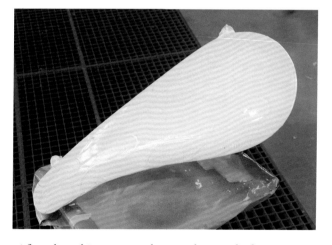

After the white sets up the panel is ready for some white pearl.

Now we spray two light coats of PPG white pearl.

Each flame can be airbrushed orange fading into yellow.

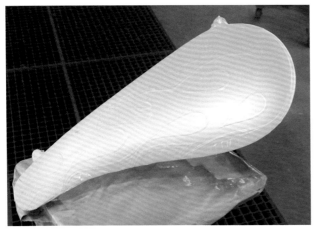

Let the pearl set up for one hour to be safe before moving on, so tape won't mark it.

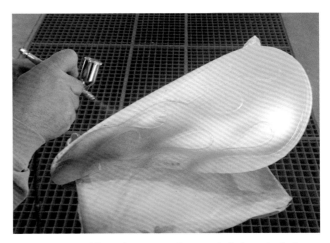

Orange should go from tips forward fading lightly.

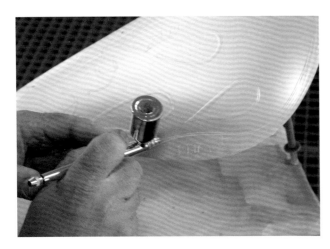

After dusting a little yellow on the front of tank, and the front of each flame, start airbrushing with orange.

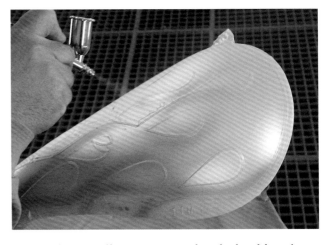

Using the DeVilbiss Dagger airbrush should make blending easy.

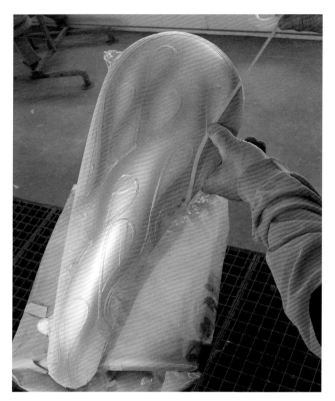

With no clear on the air brushed areas there is no room for errors.

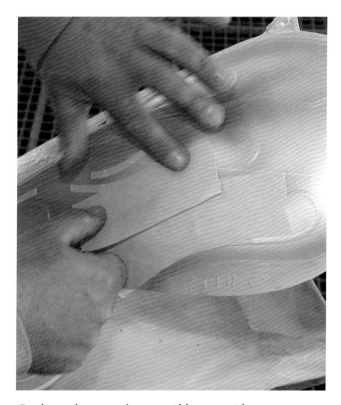

Back mask as much as possible to avoid overspray.

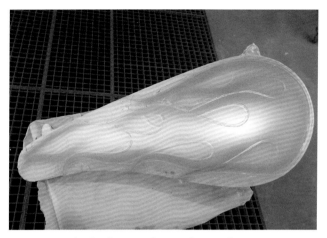

Next step shade the tips forward in red.

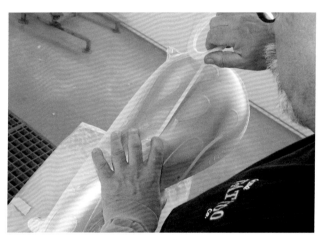

Now the crossover's only need to be taped off to get the crossover effect.

Back mask to keep overspray off the best of the flames.

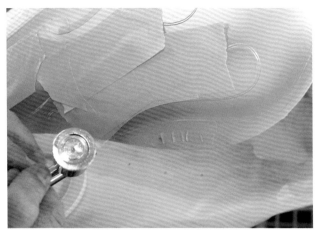

Each masked flame tip gets shaded from back to front in red.

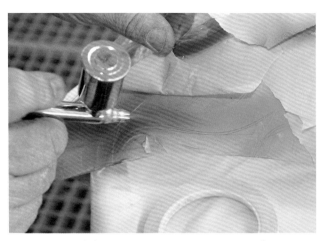

Be very careful not to get overspray on tape lines.

The red should flow right into orange with a smooth transition.

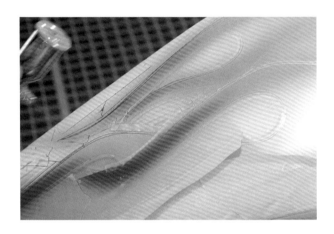

After shading is done overlay becomes very apparent.

All other tips need red shade and fade.

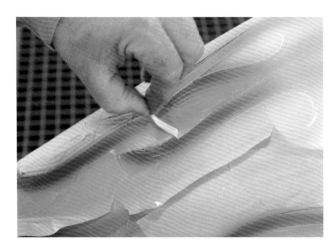

Always be careful removing tape. Pull flat as possible towards itself.

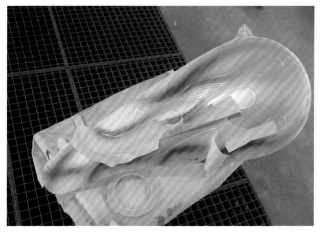

Next step is shade each tip with a little purple.

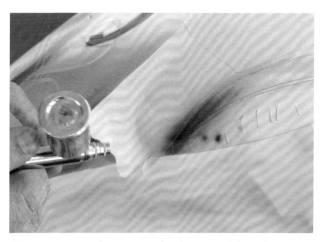

You sometimes have to go back over with red to get the purple blend right.

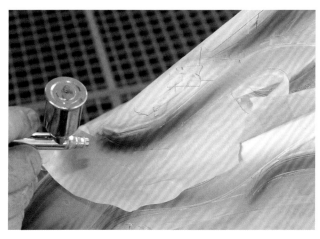

Make sure you go real easy with the purple, so as to make the blend.

Here you can see the how the flame lick fades from yellow-orange through red, to purple.

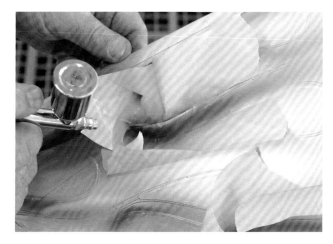

Tape all around the tip so no purple gets on the rest of the job.

You can see in this photo the purple tip needs a red into purple blend.

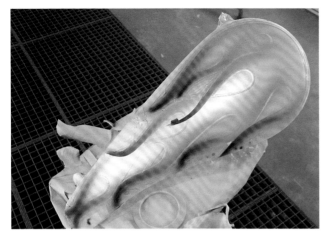

It's a good idea to step back to see if it needs more airbrush shading and blending.

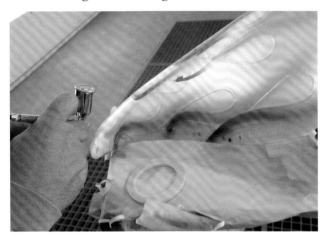

I decide to add just a little more purple.

The air nozzle will eliminate small pieces of paint at the edge of the flames.

Now the fun part, removing the tape.

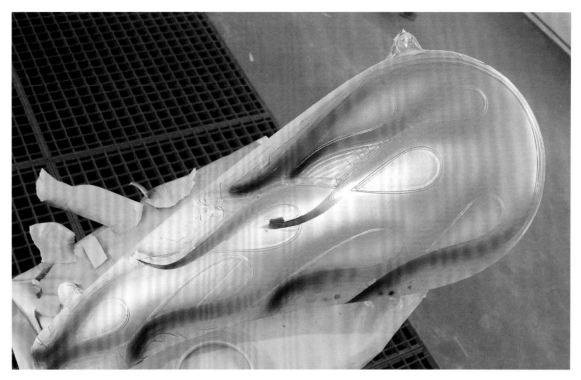

Purple adds a bright touch to the job.

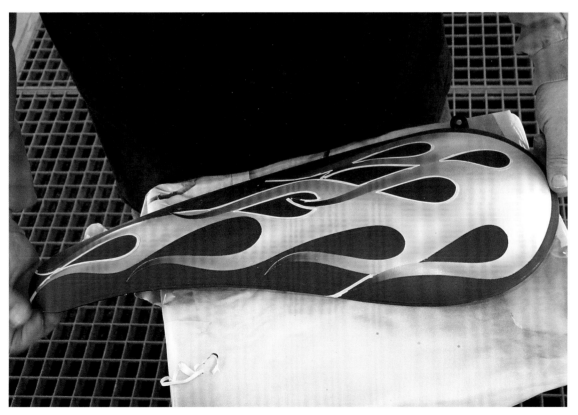

With the tape removed you can see what you've got, and hope you didn't miss a spot. Ready for clear, then striping.

ADVANCED TATTOO ART

The art of the tattoo has emerged from the garage to the parlor, from the local bar to the board room. With interest in tattoos at a high point, the time is right for a detailed look at the art, and the artists, who create the elaborate designs.

Doug Mitchel takes the reader inside the shops of ten well-known and very experienced artists spread across the country. Both a how-to book and a photo-intense look at the world or tattoos, Advanced

Tattoo Art includes interviews with the artists that explain not only how they do what they do, but their personal preference for materials and methods.

Detailed photo sequences follow each artist through a tattoo project, from the customer's concept, through the sketch and outline, to the finished and colorful design. The chapters document not only the techniques, but also the inks and tools used during each step of the process.

Ten Chapters	144 Pages	$24.95

Over 400 photos-100% color

ADV CUSTOM MOTORCYCLE ASSEMBLY & FABRICATION

No longer content to build copies of stock motorcycles, today's builder wants a motorcycle that's longer, lower and sexier than anything approved by a factory design team.

Wolfgang was there at the very beginning of the trend with their Ultimate V-Twin Motorcycle book. Today they're back with their new book, Advanced Custom Motorcycle Assembly & Fabrication. Part

catalog, part service manual and part inspiration, this new book offers help with Planning the project, getting the right look and actually assembling that custom bike you've dreamed about for years.

Three start-to-finish sequences show not just how the best bikes are bolted together, but how the unique one-off gas tanks are shaped and then covered with candy brandywine paint.

Nine Chapters	144 Pages	$24.95

Over 400 photos-100% color

HOW-TO-PAINT BARNS AND BUILDINGS

The world is filled with wooden barns and metal buildings in need of paint. Though painting a barn might seem a simple thing the sheer size of the project can intimidate even the most die-hard do-it-yourselfer.

Painting a large building requires efficient preparation, the right products and some kind of spray application of the paint. How to Paint Barns & Buildings walks the reader through the easiest way

to prep the surface, which products work best on big surfaces, and the various spray equipment options – many of which can be rented rather than purchased.

To show how easy it can be to paint a barn or a building, this new book includes two start-to-finish paint jobs, one wooden barn and one metal building. Each sequence includes all the steps and illustrates how the right paint and equipment makes it easy to paint a barn or metal building.

Nine Chapters	144 Pages	$24.95

500 color images - 100% color

BARRIS KUSTOM TECHNIQUES OF THE '50S VOL 4

Flames, Scallops, Paneling and Striping (Vol 4)
In this book George Barris explains how he and brother Sam did their custom painting and early flame jobs in the 1950s. No one can tell this story as well as George Barris, a fine photographer and the man who built many of the cars shown in the book.

People are as interesting in painting and customizing now, as they were when this material was first created, in the 1950s. Everyone wants to know

how to do a flame job, or how to run a pair of pinstripes straight down the side of their car.

This particular book contains more than just the photos and words of George Barris. This volume contains first-person side-bars by legendary painters and builders like Dean Jeffries and Larry Watson, describing how they developed their talents and what it was like to work directly with the Barris brothers.

Six Chapters	144 Pages	$24.95

Over 300 classic black & white photos

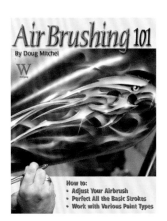

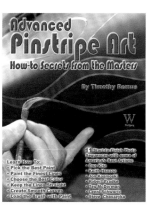

Dave Perewitz/Cycle Fab
910 Plymouth St.
Bridgewater, MA 02324
508 697 3595

PPG Industries
19699 Progress Drive
Strongsville, OH 44149 (800) 647-6050
(Customer Service) www.ppgrefinish.com

Keith Hanson
233 Canton
Stoughton, MA 02072
781 344 9166
www.hansoncustom.com

Lowell's Performance Coatings & Equipment
5251 W. 74th St.
Edina, MN 55349
952 392 6060

Pro Paint
530 10th Ave.
Baldwin, WI 54002
800 234 6898

DeVilbiss Spray Equipment
www.devilbiss.com